Molière

Le Misanthrope

David Whitton

Lecturer in French Studies
University of Lancaster

University of Glasgow French and German Publications
1991

University of Glasgow French and German Publications

Series Editors: Mark G. Ward (German)
Geoff Woollen (French)

Consultant Editors : Colin Smethurst
Kenneth Varty

Modern Languages Building, University of Glasgow,
Glasgow G12 8QL, Scotland.

Published by University of Glasgow French and German Publications, 1991

Printed by BPCC Wheatons Ltd., Exeter.

ISBN 0 85261 280 X

Contents

Preface

Students of Molière have at their disposal a wealth of criticism and, in the case of *Le Misanthrope,* almost an *embarras de richesses.* It is an enigmatic play, and since the eighteenth century has given rise to vastly differing interpretations. The play has been interpreted as a comedy, a *drame,* and a tragedy. Alceste has been seen as ridiculous, *sympathique,* grotesque, a holy fool, a tragic victim, a heroic superman... It is not my intention in this short study to review the play's critical history in detail. Students will, however, find a brief guide to it in Chapter One and in the Bibliography. Readers who require a more detailed guide should consult Michaut, *Les Luttes de Molière* (pp. 203-210) and, for an up-to-date census covering the last twenty years, M. Gutwirth's 'Visages d'Alceste'.

My excuse for adding to the literature on *Le Misanthrope* is that I think students will find use for an Introductory Guide which sets out to examine how the play works as a piece of theatre. Criticism of *Le Misanthrope* has tended to concentrate overwhelmingly on the moral issues raised by the play. Given the significance and ambiguity of the *moraliste* elements in the play, these are naturally an important focus of criticism. But it is important, too, to begin by recognising that the play is not a dramatisation of a moral thesis. It is, before anything else, a work of theatre. The aim of this study, therefore, like that of the companion volume by Noël Peacock on *L'École des femmes,* is to treat *Le Misanthrope* as a script for performance. Three quarters of it is in the form of a commentary where the play will be examined from scene to scene and from moment to moment. Given the often quite detailed nature of the analysis, it will be read most profitably by those who have already read the play closely or who have a copy of the text to hand. I shall try to show how structure, action, movement, rhythm and tone combine to create comedy, emotion and significance. The overall aim is to examine Molière's use of the theatrical medium in order to identify the nature of the dramatic experience it creates.

Quotations from the play are taken from the Despois & Mesnard edition of Molière's *Œuvres.* References to *Le Misanthrope* are given in the form of act and scene (e.g. III, 3) or line numbers alone. Notes are given in the form of bold numerals which refer to numbered items in the bibliography, followed by a page reference, where applicable (e.g. **2**, p. 10).

Chapter One

The Play and its History

Molière in 1666

Molière may have been working on *Le Misanthrope* for up to two years before it was first produced in 1666. According to Brossette, he read the first act in the presence of Boileau as early as 1664. If this is so, it was an unusually long period of composition for an overworked actor-manager who was often forced to write hurriedly to meet his company's demands for a supply of fresh material. It may help to acccount for the unusual formal and stylistic perfection for which the play is often noted.

Le Misanthrope was his sixteenth play. Molière, whose company had taken the title *Troupe du Roi* the previous year, was at the height of his popularity. Behind him lay a string of outstanding artistic achievements which had made him the most admired and controversial playwright of his age. From the time of his return to Paris in 1658 he had aimed to raise comedy from simple farce to the level of a profound art. For Molière, this meant comedy which captured universal human foibles such as pretentiousness, gullibility and all manifestations of the irrational. Like all his contemporaries, Molière was profoundly interested in human nature, and his aim, he said, was to 'entrer comme il faut dans le ridicule des hommes'. But it also meant depicting the follies of the day in plays set in a recognisable contemporary social milieu. *Les Précieuses ridicules* (1659), a play in which topical satire of manners and comedy of character are grafted on to the traditional situations of farce, signalled the appearance of this new type of comedy. As his art developed, he became increasingly audacious in tackling the burning social and philosophical issues of the day. He also became the leading Court entertainer in the 1660s. It is worth remembering, though, that it was as a *farceur* that he was most acclaimed by the people. The most popular by far of his plays during his lifetime was the farce *Sganarelle ou le Cocu imaginaire*.

For Molière, the years between 1664 and 1666 were a period of astonishing creativity. As well as *La Princesse d'Élide,* a *comédie-ballet* which was devised for a Court entertainment, he produced four new plays, very different in kind one from the other and each a masterpiece of its genre: *Tartuffe,* a satire of religious hypocrisy, and the most frequently performed comedy of the entire French repertoire; *Dom Juan,* a disturbing and enigmatic treatment of a modern legend; *Le Médecin malgré lui,* a traditional farce often considered to be the finest of all French farces, and *Le Misanthrope,* the most sophisticated of his comedies and held by many to be the summit of French comedy.

The background to this explosion of creative originality was a period in which Molière was beset by personal and professional difficulties. His only son died in 1664. Rumours started to circulate about the infidelities of his young wife Armande—a circumstance which enemies (and some later critics) claimed he dramatised in the relationship between Alceste and Célimène. 1664 also saw the onset of the 'Querelle de *Tartuffe*' and the start of a five-year struggle to get that play staged. This was the second great controversy to result from Molière's ambition of raising comedy to the level of a moral issue. (The first was over *L'École des femmes* in 1662-3). The following year, 1665, *Dom Juan* had to be taken off after only fifteen performances. The circumstances are unclear, but *L'École des femmes* and *Tartuffe* had earned Molière many enemies. It is possible that the coalition of *dévots,* prudes and theatrical rivals succeeded in suppressing it. By the end of 1665 Molière was already seriously ill due to the constant pressure of his work. The year ended with a double professional blow: a rupture with Racine when the latter, having promised his new play *Alexandre* to Molière, handed it as well to the rival company at the Hôtel de Bourgogne; and, ten days later, the death of the Queen Mother Anne of Austria causing theatres to be closed in mourning for two months.

When performances resumed in February 1666, the company's programme included plays by Corneille (*Sertorius, Le Menteur*) and other popular authors of the day such as Scarron, Desmarets and de Visé, together with stock items from Molière's own repertoire: *Les Précieuses ridicules, Les Fâcheux, L'Amour médecin, L'Ecole des maris* and *Le Cocu imaginaire.* At this stage in his career Molière could not be expected to supply all the material for his company to perform, nor would this have been commercially wise. Nevertheless, after the suppression of *Tartuffe* and the rapid closure of *Dom Juan,* the need for a new play to revive a somewhat stale programme must have been very pressing. *Le Misanthrope* had its first performance at the Palais Royal theatre on 4 June 1666. Lancaster speculates that Molière completed the writing by the end of 1665 but chose to delay the play's launch until the end of the period of Court mourning (**9**, p. 654). This seems difficult to reconcile with the fact, first, that he gave a full programme of performances throughout March and into April, and second, that even when the new season began after Easter, it was still four weeks before *Le Misanthrope* appeared on the bill. Even then, the Court, which was in residence at Fontainebleau, was still officially in mourning. As a result, a play whose subject matter might have been expected to hold special appeal for the King had to open without a royal presence. It has been plausibly suggested that this may have prejudiced the success of the new play, though contemporary accounts indicate that there was a strong compensatory presence of members of the Court at Molière's town theatre. Surprisingly, *Le Misanthrope* was one of the few plays by Molière never performed at Court.

The play's reception

There has long been a belief that *Le Misanthrope* was a flop. Grimarest (writing, it must be remembered, forty years after the event) claimed that '[Molière] sentit dès la première représentation que le peuple de Paris voulait plus rire qu'admirer', that 'la seconde représentation fut encore plus faible que la première' and that 'La troisième représentation fut encore moins heureuse que les précédentes' (**25**, pp. 57-8). Louis Racine, in his *Mémoires,* also speaks of 'la première représentation [...] qui fut très malheureuse' (**1**, p. 361), and Voltaire claimed that 'le théâtre fut désert dès le troisième jour' (*ibid.*). Modern editors, more guardedly, have described it as 'un succès honnête, sans plus', a 'succès d'estime', and 'un demi-succès' (see **37**).

Grimarest is also the source of an enduring legend, that Molière was only to able to save *Le Misanthrope* from folding by the showman's expedient of coupling it in a double bill with his new and extremely popular farce, *Le Médecin malgré lui*: 'Il ne fut pas plus tôt rentré dans son cabinet qu'il travailla au *Médecin malgré lui*, pour soutenir *Le Misanthrope*' (**25**, p. 57). It is a seductive story but is contradicted by the facts. *Le Misanthrope* was played on its own during July and August. *Le Médecin malgré lui* was first performed throughout August in conjunction not with *Le Misanthrope* but with other plays. It was only in September, after *Le Misanthrope* had completed its first run, that the two plays were performed on the same bill.

Some evidence of the play's fortunes is provided by Molière's fellow-actor and company archivist La Grange, who kept records of performance dates and takings. In theory it should be possible to compare the records for *Le Misanthrope* with those of other new plays. In practice, his *Registre* is difficult to interpret unequivocally. So many special factors intervene (holidays, seasonal variations in patterns of theatregoing, etc.) that direct comparison with other plays is difficult. However, the facts are as follows: during its initial solo run between 4 June and 1 August the play had 21 performances—significantly fewer than *Tartuffe* (28), *L'École des femmes* (31) or *Les Précieuses ridicules* (33), though better than *Les Femmes savantes* (19), *Dom Juan* (15) or *L'Avare* (9). Since the average number of performances on initial runs for all Molière's plays has been calculated at 23 (**37**, p. 145), there is no evidence here for *Le Misanthrope* having been the flop that Grimarest claimed. Nor do the box-office takings indicate that it was a financial failure. It is true that the *Registre* shows a sharp decline in takings on the third performance (886 *livres*, compared with 1447 *livres* and 1617 *livres* for the first two performances). But such a pattern was not uncommon. To understand its significance, it has to be remembered not only that the première of a new play by Molière was a major event for Paris society, but also that prices for some categories of tickets were doubled for the first performances. Lower receipts for subsequent performances, therefore, do not necessarily mean fewer spectators. On the tenth performance, given on a Sunday (normally the most popular theatre-going day), *Le Misanthrope* brought in only 212 *livres*, and this has been used to provide evidence of a great failure. However, this figure should not be taken in isolation. The previous Friday saw takings of 601 *livres*, and receipts climbed again to 349 *livres* on the following Tuesday.

Summarising a complex picture, then, Christopher Gossip may well be correct to conclude that 'there would appear to be no need to apologize for the reception given to *Le Misanthrope* in 1666' (**37**, p. 148). The two main indicators—length of run and box-office takings—show the success of *Le Misanthrope* to have been average but by no means disastrous.

Turning from the number of spectators to how those spectators received the play, it has been said that *Le Misanthrope* did not enjoy either the enthusiastic acclaim or the widely-based popular support that greeted Molière's most successful plays. 'Un applaudissement général, populaire, n'avait pas été d'abord obtenu' (**1**, p. 365); 'Devant une œuvre assez neuve, les contemporains hésitèrent' (**6**, p. 355); 'On sait en effet quel accueil hésitant les contemporains de Molière, dans leur grande majorité, réservèrent au *Misanthrope'* (**34**, p. 580). Here we are on firmer ground. Contemporary accounts all affirm that the play was admired in Court circles, as one might expect with a comedy dealing with high-society manners. The lack of reference to other sectors of the audience may tell its own story. In *La Muse Dauphine* of 17 June 1666, Subligny wrote: '*Toute la cour* en dit du bien' (**1**, p. 357: my italics). De Visé makes a similar distinction when he reports that '*les courtisans* ont assez fait voir par leurs applaudissements qu'ils trouvaient la comédie belle' (**1**, p. 441: my italics). De Visé's *Lettre écrite sur la comédie du Misanthrope* is the fullest contemporary account of the play we possess. Its aim is to praise the new play, but a careful reading between the lines suggests that *Le Misanthrope* was not without its detractors: 'Je pourrois vous dire en deux mots', he writes, 'qu'il a plu, et que son intention étant de plaire, les critiques ne peuvent pas dire qu'il ait mal fait' (**1**, p. 430). A more explicit reference to the play's less than enthusiastic reception comes when he refers to the confrontation between Alceste and Célimène in IV, 3: 'Je ne crois pas que les beautés de cette scène soient connues de tous ceux qui l'ont vue représenter: elle est trop délicatement traitée; mais je puis assurer que tout le monde a remarqué qu'elle étoit bien écrite, et que *les personnes d'esprit* en ont bien su connoître les finesses' (**1**, p. 438: my italics). This suggestion that the scene was too subtle to be immediately appreciated by everyone may well be relevant to the play as a whole.

The most discriminating critics, such as Boileau, already identified *Le Misanthrope* as an incomparable achievement. As for the *parterre,* Grimarest was probably very near to the truth when he said that 'le peuple de Paris voulait plus rire qu'admirer.' In short, *Le Misanthrope* seems to have been a play for connoisseurs. If this was indeed the case in 1666, it is remarkable how little has changed over three centuries. Admired for its unrivalled subtlety, psychological depth and classical perfection, no-one would claim for it the euphoric laughter-making appeal of, say, *L'École des femmes* or *Le Bourgeois gentilhomme.* In terms of numbers of productions, its popularity has been uncannily consistent over the centuries. With none of the peaks and troughs that have brought other comedies into fashion and out again, it has maintained a steady place around the fourth position in Molière's repertoire: statistics compiled by the Comédie-Française at the tercentenary of Molière's death show that, up to 1973, *Le Misanthrope* had 2001 performances. The three most popular plays were *Tartuffe* (3007), *L'Avare* (2367) and *Le Médecin malgré lui* (2177).

A controversial masterpiece

For many people, *Le Misanthrope* is Molière's greatest comedy, and perhaps the greatest of all comedies. Its subtlety, complexity and suggestive power place it in a class of its own. Within the confines of its limited social canvas, it succeeds in conveying an impression of the human condition in all its ambiguity and complexity, making the play appear as a summation of Molière's vision.

That we are in the presence of a masterpiece there can be no doubt. It was recognised as such from the moment it first appeared. On 17 June 1666—barely two weeks after the first performance—Subligny wrote in *La Muse Dauphine:* 'Après son *Misanthrope* il ne faut plus voir rien; / C'est un chef-d'œuvre inimitable' (**10**, p. 267). Another verse gazetteer, Robinet, had already declared:

> *Le Misanthrope* enfin se joue:
> Je le vis dimanche, et j'avoue
> Que de Molière, son auteur,
> N'a rien fait de cette hauteur.
>
> (*Lettre à Madame,* 12 June 1666)

Grimarest, Molière's first biographer—though admittedly

not an entirely reliable source—even attributed the same sentiment to the author himself: '"sûrement je ne ferai pas mieux", disait Molière à tout le monde' (**25**, p. 58). In the eighteenth century, Voltaire reported that 'L'Europe regarde cet ouvrage comme le chef-d'œuvre du haut comique' (**1**, p. 426). Rousseau, who detested the play for its immorality, also agreed that 'on [la] reconnaît unanimement pour son chef-d'œuvre' (**11**, p. 47). Modern critics have been no less reticent in placing it at the very summit of Molière's achievement. Jasinski, in his influential study of *Le Misanthrope,* held it to be 'un chef-d'œuvre unique [...] une des réussites les plus parfaites de l'art classique' (**17**, p. 326).

At the same time, *Le Misanthrope* is also the play which has most divided later critics: not between admirers and detractors, but between those who see the play's qualities in a form of pure comedy, and those who consider it to be something more than a comedy, a comedy which goes beyond the comic into territory bordering the tragic. The question is partly a matter of tone. Is it a comedy or a serious play, or even, as Brunetière claimed, a *tragédie bourgeoise?* De Visé recognised that it was not a comedy which provoked easy laughter. In a felicitious and much-quoted phrase, he said it gave rise to 'le rire dans l'âme' (**1**, p. 440). Many people have sensed a melancholic tone to *Le Misanthrope,* and for some the satire has a dark and bitter flavour; Jacques Arnavon, for instance, considered the play to be 'un grondement gigantesque' (**19**, p. 195).

A perennial question is whether Alceste himself is a comic character, and if so, what sort of comic character. It is here that critical opinion is most divided. If most commentators feel that there is something ridiculous in Alceste's behaviour, this has not prevented others from being conscious above all of the poignant side of the character. Sainte-Beuve, while stopping short of a full-blown tragic interpretation, saw that Molière had pushed comedy to the very edge of tragedy. Alceste, he said, represented 'ce qu'il y a de plus sérieux, de plus noble, de plus élevé dans le comique, le point où le ridicule confine au courage, à la vertu. Une ligne plus haut, et le comique cesse, et on a un personnage purement généreux, presque héroïque et tragique' (*Portraits littéraires,* IV). But for many nineteenth-century Romantics, the hero's suffering was nothing short of tragic. Performances of the period emphasised the subjective suffering of the central character.

Duvicquet, after witnessing such a performance, wrote: 'N'est-on pas plus près des larmes que de la gaieté lorsque le vertueux Alceste foudroie de ses reproches, presque tragiquement exprimées, la perfidie de l'indigne coquette qui se joue de sa bonne foi?' (*Journal des Débats,* 19 décembre 1823). Musset, also responding to an evening at the Comédie-Française, shed a tear for Alceste's ' [...] mâle gaîté, si triste et si profonde / Que, lorsqu'on vient d'en rire, on devrait en pleurer!' ('Une Soirée perdue', 1840). An important body of criticism in the nineteenth century (but now viewed with suspicion) attached importance to the subjective side of Molière's writing. Interpretation of his plays laid great stress on biographical circumstances such as his unhappy marriage to Armande Béjart. For this school, *Le Misanthrope* was an autobiographical confession, the anguished outpouring of a tormented author: 'Pauvre Molière! toutes les souffrances qu'il n'osait avouer, il les a écrites de ses larmes, dans ce beau tableau de son ménage et du cœur humain qu'il a nommé, mal à propos, *Le Misanthrope'* (Loève-Veimars, *Journal des Débats,* 6 mai 1839).

A further strand of opinion sees Alceste as both comic and tragic. It has been argued (e.g. by C. S. Gutkind) that he is comic in his relation with society, and tragic in his doomed love for Célimène. Others have seen this as a sign that the play is flawed by a fundamental ambiguity which Molière himself was unable to resolve. For Edmond Schérer, the play is an artistic failure. He argued that Molière, having conceived Alceste initially as a noble and attractive character, then subjected him to comic distortions which destroyed the primary coherence of the role (*Études sur la littérature contemporaine,* VIII, Paris, 1885). In a variation on this line, Professor Yarrow also speculates that Molière lost sight of his original intention, causing his attitude to Alceste to shift (**57**). Unlike Schérer, however, Yarrow detects a shift from an initially comic Alceste in Act I to a more admirable, quasi-tragic figure in Act V.

Ultimately the question is not simply one of tone and genre but of what Molière intended to say in *Le Misanthrope.* What is the play's lesson? indeed, does it seek to convey any lesson at all? There are as many answers as there are critics. Without going into every nuance, still less attempting to answer each point, the contours of the debate can be outlined thus:

1) For some, Alceste stands for an ideal of absolute sincerity. His principles, although carried to excess, are noble ones; his criticisms of his fellow men, although intemperately expressed, are justified. Viewed from this perspective, Alceste is the hero of the play, and an object of sympathy and admiration. His idealism is contrasted favourably both with the insincerity of most of the other characters, and with the more insidiously complacent attitude of Philinte. If he is sometimes guilty of excess, this is fully justified, because 'il faut demander beaucoup pour obtenir quelque chose' (de Visé, **1**, p. 440).

In this connection, special mention must be made of Rousseau, whose charge of immorality against *Le Misanthrope* had a lasting influence on perceptions of the play. Rousseau accused Molière of ridiculing virtue. He took it as axiomatic that Alceste was a virtuous and admirable character (a point which some would dispute), and found it intolerable that Molière should have mocked such a character:

> Vous ne sauriez me nier deux choses: l'une, qu'Alceste, dans cette pièce, est un homme droit, sincère, estimable, un véritable homme de bien; l'autre, que l'auteur lui donne un personnage ridicule. C'en est assez, ce me semble, pour rendre Molière inexcusable. (**11**, p. 48)

The same logic led him to see Philinte, his more compliant friend, as an unprincipled scoundrel. In the philosopher and critic's view, he was:

> un de ces honnêtes gens du grand monde dont les maximes ressemblent beaucoup à celles des fripons; de ces gens si doux, si modérées, qui trouvent toujours que tout va bien, parce qu'ils ont intérêt que rien n'aille mieux; qui sont toujours contents de tout le monde, parce qu'ils ne se soucient de personne... (**11**, p. 51)

Admittedly, Rousseau (a great admirer of Molière's art) had a particular aim in this. The *Lettre à d'Alembert sur les spectacles* was part of a broad campaign against what he saw as the frivolous and immoral tendencies of literature and theatre generally. His denunciation of *Le Misanthrope,* therefore, was not disinterested criticism but an attempt to use it as a polemical weapon. There seems no doubt that his own deep convictions (and lack of humour) also led him personally to identify with Alceste. Nevertheless his indignation has struck a chord with other idealists, who see Alceste as the hero of a moral crusade.

2) For other readers, the truth is the exact opposite. Rather than personifying a cult of virtue, Alceste is seen above all as an *atrabilaire*. This interpretation highlights the comedy of 'humours', about which more will be said later (see below, pp. 14, 19). Conversely Philinte, far from being a shallow cynic, is the model of the seventeenth-century social and moral ideal of reasonable *honnêteté,* and Molière's spokesman in the play. This approach includes the 'Raisonneur' school of criticism, which seeks to identify Molière's message in a character who embodies the voice of reason and moderation. Philinte, like Alceste, recognises the defects of human nature. However, he responds not by futile ranting but by phlegmatic acceptance of the inevitable. In his dealings with his fellows, he exercises tolerance, courtesy and tact—qualities which we are meant to see not as unprincipled but as positive social virtues. Napoleon was especially sensitive to Philinte's qualities. 'C'est un homme raisonnable', he is reported as saying, 'honnête, de bonne compagnie, et incapable de la moindre action ou du moindre discours qui blesserait la morale ou la délicatesse' (*Mémoires de Bausset,* II, p.184). Measured against this yardstick, Alceste appears less as an idealist than as an irascible, egocentric *inadapté.* Against a background of social satire, then, the play would suggest an 'art of living'—both positively, by depicting its incarnation in Philinte and Éliante, and negatively, in the portrayal of someone in whom it is comically lacking.

3) Attempting to reconcile these extremes, it has been argued that neither Alceste's bile nor Philinte's phlegm is presented as a model for approval. Alceste is fundamentally right in his principles but wrong in pursuing them so extravagantly, while Philinte exhibits the qualities of tolerance and sociability that his friend lacks, but is complacent in his acceptance of social vices. In other words, we are presented with two types of excess: excessive flexibility and excessive inflexibility, excessive indulgence and excessive intolerance. Reason, therefore, suggests that the ideal behaviour would involve a synthesis of the qualities represented by Alceste and Philinte that avoids the excesses of both.

4) In all the above interpretations, it is assumed that the play involves a clash of principles or modes of behaviour, framed in a perspective which invites us to choose between

them. This rests on a belief that Molière was primarily motivated by a reforming ideal. Hence Adam writes: 'Molière a voulu travailler à la correction des mœurs. [...] Une grande idée l'inspirait: sa foi dans la vocation morale du théâtre' (**6**, p. 407). However, a more recent spectrum of opinion has rejected the whole notion of his theatre as an 'école des mœurs', and highlighted instead the comic or theatrical procedures from which Molière's comedies spring. For René Bray, what motivates Molière is not a reforming mission but a comic vocation. His choice and treatment of dramatic material must, therefore, be understood in terms of the comic possibilities it offered. Hence: 'L'intention de Molière, la pensée qui donne à son œuvre la force et l'unité, ce n'est pas une pensée de moraliste, c'est une intention d'artiste. [...] Quand il peint Tartuffe ou Dom Juan, le poète cherche non pas à ridiculiser un hypocrite ou un libertin, mais à en dégager la force comique' (**20**, pp. 32 & 30). In this perspective, *Le Misanthrope* would not be a didactic theorem but a comic clash of opposing forces expressed in action. Molière's so-called ideas, in fact, may be nothing more than the ideas necessary for the dramatic contrast.

Surveying these varied critical perspectives, one is tempted to conclude that they tell us more about the critics and the preoccupations of their time than about the play. This is natural enough, since great works of art have no fixed 'meaning': their significance changes according to the vantage point of the viewer. It is quite possible that post-Romantic sensibility makes it difficult for modern spectators to view Alceste's trials with the degree of detachment necessary to achieve a balanced view of the play. The best evidence we have of what Molière's contemporaries thought is that Alceste was ridiculous but not unattractive, *sympathique* but not *pathéthique*. According to de Visé, 'Le Misanthrope, malgré sa folie, si l'on peut ainsi appeler son humeur, a le caractère d'un honnête homme, et beaucoup de fermeté [...] bien qu'il paroisse en quelque façon ridicule, il dit des choses fort justes' (**1**, p. 440). But one thing that seems never to have occurred to anyone in the seventeenth century was to consider that Alceste was *tragic.*

Three centuries of criticism confirm that *Le Misanthrope* is an unusually rich and possibly ambiguous work of art, capable of sustaining a multitude of different interpretations. This, as it happens, is a defining characteristic of what we consider to be a masterpiece. Ultimately we are left confronting the play itself. In the ensuing chapters I shall suggest a reading of the text, focusing on Molière's handling of the medium of theatre and trying as objectively as possible to see how it works on spectators and what kind of dramatic experience it creates.

Chapter Two

The Composition of the Play

The play's conception

We shall never know what Molière's intentions were when he wrote *Le Misanthrope.* Nevertheless, it will help us to interpret the play more clearly if we try to form a mental model of its conception.

As we have seen, criticism of *Le Misanthrope* has focused largely on Alceste. This is inevitable, given his towering presence in the play and the ambivalence of the role. It may be, however, that Molière's starting point, and the play's *idée maîtresse,* was not Alceste at all, but some other idea. One way to account for the play, I suggest, is to reason as follows:

1) To begin with, we should think of *Le Misanthrope* not primarily as a comedy of a character-type, like *L'Avare* or *Le Malade imaginaire,* but as a comedy of manners portraying high Parisian society. In *L'Impromptu de Versailles* (1663), Molière had envisaged the satirical possibilities of a broad tableau of society. In terms which clearly anticipate some of the characters of *Le Misanthrope,* he says of himself (sc. 4):

> Crois-tu qu'il ait épuisé dans ses comédies tout le ridicule des hommes? Et, sans sortir de la cour, n'a-t-il pas encore vingt caractères de gens où il n'a point touché? N'a-t-il pas, par exemple, ceux qui se font les plus grandes amitiés du monde, et qui, le dos tourné, font galanterie de se déchirer l'un l'autre? N'a-t-il pas ces adulateurs à outrance, ces flatteurs insipides ... ceux qui caressent également tout le monde, qui promènent leurs civilités à droite et à gauche, et courent à tous ceux qu'ils voient avec les mêmes embrassades et les mêmes protestations d'amitié?

Surely *Le Misanthrope* is just such a comedy. De Visé, the source closest to the author himself, affirms that Molière conceived the play as a satire of contemporary manners: 'Il n'a point voulu faire une comédie pleine d'incidents, mais une pièce seulement *où il pût parler contre les mœurs du siècle'* (**1**, p. 430: my italics). From this as a starting point, other elements fall more readily into place and the play becomes less of an enigma.

2) In order to give focus to the satire—what could be more natural?—he puts the criticism in the mouth of an enemy of society, i.e. a misanthropist. That Alceste is Molière's spokesman for an attack on contemporary society seems undeniable, for whatever one may think of the way he voices them, his criticisms are objectively justified from within the play itself. How this is affected by a comic interpretation of the role is a question we shall come to shortly. It is important to note, though, that Alceste supplies only one line of attack. Philinte, in his contrasting way, provides a second. While regarding Alceste's reforming crusade as 'une folie à nulle autre seconde', he shares Alceste's fundamental analysis of society and human nature. ('Oui, je vois ces défauts, dont votre âme murmure, Comme vices unis à l'humaine nature', 173-4). As a result, much of what he says serves to reinforce Alceste's criticisms of humankind. Thirdly, and most ingeniously, Molière completes the attack by coupling Alceste with a *médisante.* Célimène's role is often described in terms of the contrast it provides with that of Alceste—the comic paradox of the champion of sincerity haplessly in love with a coquette. This is an important part of the picture, yet where criticism of society is concerned Célimène is the ideal *accomplice* of Alceste. By making her not only a coquette but also a *médisante,* Molière introduces a Trojan horse wittily satirising her own set. For de Visé, the idea was one of brilliant, self-evident simplicity:

> l'on doit admirer que, dans une pièce où Molière veut parler contre les mœurs du siècle et n'épargner personne, il nous fait voir une médisante avec un ennemi des hommes. Je vous laisse à penser si ces deux personnes ne peuvent pas naturellement parler contre toute la terre, puisque l'un hait les hommes, et que l'autre se plaît à en dire tout le mal qu'elle en sait. (**1**, p. 431)

The satirical scheme, then, involves a three-pronged attack, the *misanthrope,* the *honnête homme* and the *médisante,* providing three complementary perspectives on 'les mœurs du siècle'. Eliante provides support for Philinte's position. The other characters, Oronte, Arsinoé, the two *marquis,* have only to be themselves in order to condemn themselves.

3) Returning to Alceste, had Molière endowed him with a reasoned, detached misanthropy, the play could hardly have

been comic. A rational misanthropist would turn it into a sententious morality play, as we can see by imagining Philinte as the central character. Artistic necessity requires Molière to redress matters by drawing Alceste back on to comic territory. Accordingly he makes him an *atrabilaire,* thereby deforming misanthropy into a comic disorder. At a stroke, he singles himself out not by his admirable ideas but by his *bizarrerie.* He becomes peevish, petulant, humourless, an object of curiosity and derision. In the context of seventeenth-century *honnêteté,* Alceste's individualism can only be a comic failing. A contemporary treatise on courtly manners gives the maxim 'N'être pas trop singulier, ni par affectation ni par inadvertance', and warns:

> Quelques gens se font remarquer par leur singularité, c'est-à-dire, par des actions de folie, qui sont plutôt des défauts que des différences. [...] Il ne sert à rien de se singulariser, sinon à se faire passer pour un original impertinent. Ce qui provoque alternativement la moquerie des uns, et la mauvaise humeur des autres. (*L'Homme de cour,* 1684)

The writer could almost have been thinking of Alceste, whose 'singularité' only too plainly provokes 'la moquerie des uns' (Philinte, Célimène, Clitandre, Acaste) and 'la mauvaise humeur des autres' (Oronte).

4) The consequence of making Alceste a comic figure is inevitably to undermine his moral position. One begins to see why critics such as Bray have questioned the whole notion of Molière motivated by a clearly defined polemical stance. In *Le Misanthrope* he gives us the awkward (for some) proposition of an advocate for sincerity portrayed as a figure of ridicule. Readers such as Rousseau may find this intolerable; others may prefer to conclude that Molière has chosen to remain true to the exigences of the comic stage rather than to an abstract moral thesis.

The structure and unity of the play

More than most plays, *Le Misanthrope* is very resistant to analysis of its separate elements. Like an orchestral symphony, it can only be grasped in its entirety by experiencing it as it unfolds. Although different characters and motifs hold our attention at successive moments, they interlace in an intricate way and eventually merge into one indissoluble subject.

The play combines a number of interlocking elements. The central *theme* deals with the social and moral question of hypocrisy and sincerity; there is the *portrayal of salon life* where the action takes place; woven into both of these is a more traditional comic subject, the *jealous lover motif;* there is an *action* with a double focus concerning the outcome of Alceste's relationship with Célimène and with society as a whole; and there is a plot or *intrigue* (i.e. a series of actions and incidents) arising out of the various rivalries: Oronte's quarrel with Alceste, Arsinoé's quarrel with Célimène, the rivalry between Clitandre and Acaste, Alceste's lawsuit. It is from the combination of all these elements that a dramatic structure and also patterns of meaning arise.

By 'structure' we mean the various parts of the play and the way they relate to each other. At its simplest this means the grouping of the characters, and the arrangements of the events which form the plot. And yet *Le Misanthrope* is obviously much more than a gallery of portraits and a succession of incidents. Its organisational principle depends less on a plot than on a central idea, which rests on the depiction of a social milieu. It is here, therefore, that we should begin.

Milieu

Unusually for Molière, the play is concerned exclusively with high society. Within his narrow canvas Molière gives a wide-ranging impression of a social class as a whole. We are shown the various types that inhabit the fringes of Court life, and see their daily life, their pursuits and their values. But it remains a strictly limited sector of seventeenth-century society. So it is plainly wrong to claim, as did Rigal, that '*Le Misanthrope,* ce n'est rien de moins qu'une étude presque complète de la société contemporaine et de l'humanité' (*Molière* [Paris, 1908], vol 2, p. 51). That is to take the characters at their own inflated self-estimation. Part of the point of the play is to show up the narcissism of a ruling class whose lesser members have an exaggerated idea of their own importance.

In comedies set in middle-class households, (*Tartuffe, L'Avare, Le Malade imaginaire,* etc.) it is natural that the action should involve family relationships and be centred on a paterfamilias. In *Le Misanthrope,* equally naturally, what counts is social relationships. At the centre of the play is the couple Alceste-Célimène. Around them are gathered the other characters in a series of groupings. Philinte is Alceste's friend, and also Eliante's suitor. Eliante is Célimène's cousin, and also loves Alceste and Philinte. Oronte is Célimène's suitor, and becomes Alceste's adversary. Arsinoé is Célimène's 'friend' and also loves Alceste. From this emerges a complex pattern of symmetries involving pairs of characters (Célimène-Alceste, Alceste-Philinte, Philinte-Eliante, Eliante-Alceste, Célimène-Arsinoé, Arsinoé-Alceste, Acaste-Clitandre, Alceste-Oronte, and even, behind the scenes, Oronte-Arsinoé) and triangular relationships (Alceste-Célimène-Arsinoé, Alceste-Philinte-Eliante). Our attention is constantly shifting from one set of characters to another as the groupings form, dissolve and re-form like a rondo. The action grows out of this network of friendships and rivalries.

Plot

The plot is so slight that it is sometimes claimed to be non-existent. Schlegel compared *Le Misanthrope* unfavourably with other plays by Molière, and said 'l'intrigue est encore moins animée, ou plutôt il n'y en a pas du tout' (**17**, p. 276). Another critic, Nisard, claimed that 'l'intrigue n'existe que dans la tête de certains commentateurs qui ne souffrent pas de comédie sans intrigue' (*ibid.*).

If there is a plot, it centres on Alceste. According to Lancaster, 'the plot is largely concerned with the love of three women for Alceste and the reasons for his decision not to marry any of them' (**9**, p. 657). The director Louis Jouvet found a plot, of sorts, in the long-delayed quarrel with Célimène: 'C'est la comédie d'un homme qui veut avoir un entretien décisif avec une femme qu'il aime, et qui au bout de la journée n'y est pas parvenu' (**23**, p. 90). Both these issues are important dramatic motifs but they seem to me to be subsumed in the central issue which, as I have suggested, is Alceste's relationship with Célimène and his relationship with society as a whole. It is the business of the plot to act upon, and ultimately to resolve, these twin matters. The two questions are, of course, inseparable, since the outcome of the former helps to determine the outcome of the latter.

Normally, one would expect the central character to play a leading role in shaping the course of events. *Le Misanthrope* is unusual in this respect. Because it is Alceste's fate to be constantly frustrated, we have a protagonist who is more acted upon than active. Alceste takes only one decision in the course of the play, at the very end when he finally resolves to abandon Célimène and quit society. (And even the finality of that decision is in doubt). Except for the outcome of the lawsuit, which Alceste brings upon himself by his *refusal* to act, the incidents all come about as result of action taken by secondary characters. Oronte's resentment against Alceste as a result of their quarrel leads to a series of repercussions throughout the play: the summons to appear before the *maréchaux,* the letter from Célimène which he passes to Arsinoé, his proposal of marriage to Célimène in V, 2. Arsinoé uses the letter in an attempt to discredit Célimène in Alceste's eyes and so win him for herself. Acaste and Clitandre unwittingly provoke the dénouement through their rivalry for Célimène which leads to the disclosure of her multiple infidelities. These are the meneurs du jeu. But ultimately everything comes back to Alceste. He is indirectly the source of the action, either because he provokes the actions of others, or because their actions have him as their focus. And their actions in turn help to precipitate his final decision.

We can see also how the nature of the action is shaped by the social environment. Firstly, Célimène's salon, like a miniature replica of Court society, is a closed microcosm where the lives and actions of each individual are inextricably enmeshed in those of their fellows. Secondly, it is a petty but fiercely competitive society where passions are expended on rivalries, vendettas and self-advancement. Thirdly, it is a society of hypocrites where people do not act openly, and where the seemingly aimless round of social visits masks personal interests and hidden motives. These mechanisms into built into the fabric of the play. We do not see the *meneurs du jeu* in action: instead, they operate off-stage, between the acts, and what we see is the consequences of their actions. Encounters which at the time seem to be isolated incidents are later seen to have repercussions (such as the original Alceste-Oronte quarrel) or to have had a hidden causality (such as Arsinoé's visit to Célimène). Often the result is the opposite of that intended. (Arsinoé's disclosure to Alceste of Célimène's letter to Oronte has the effect of provoking Alceste to propose to *Éliante!*). Or the effect is disproportionate to the cause. (The pact agreed by two inconsequential *petits marquis* brings down the whole pack of cards). So the plot advances surreptitiously. Only in retrospect can we see the implacable logic that binds it all together.

The result of weaving an intrigue from multiple rivalries and subterfuge is an action which is more subtle, and arguably more realistic, than conventional linear plots such as those of *Tartuffe* and *L'Avare*. The attendant danger is that it is also less vigorous and potentially diffuse. Molière compensates for this in two ways. One is the device of the delayed quarrel with Célimène, establishing a pattern of frustration which spans the first four acts. The other is the rhythmic patterning of the material to give a series of dramatic high points. It is not by accident that the most memorable climactic scenes are strategically situated, one in each of the five acts: the *scène du sonnet* in Act I, the *scène des portraits* in Act II, the Célimène-Arsinoé quarrel in Act III, the Alceste-Célimène quarrel in Act IV, and the *scène des lettres* in Act V. These moments of theatrical intensity—which do not necessarily correspond to key phases in the plot—resemble the operatic device of the aria. They provide a succession of climaxes which give the play a strong and pleasing dramatic structure independently of the plot.

Characters

'Character' is a difficult concept to delimit in Molière's theatre. It is true that one of his greatest artistic achievements is to have created compelling illusions of character. But of course these are not real people, nor do they exist independently of the situations in which we see them. They exist only insofar as they reveal themselves through speech and action. The proper place to discuss the characters, therefore, is in the Commentary; here they can be studied in the context in which they are presented. The notes below are intended only to situate them, and should not be read as 'character studies'.

Like the plot, the characters are also determined by their social milieu. Each character corresponds to a type drawn from high society: the misanthrope, the coquette, the *honnête homme,* the *honnête femme,* the prude, the courtier. They are all to some extent bounded by their character type, though to vastly differing degrees. Acaste and Clitandre are vivid but one-dimensional caricatures; at the other extreme, we have immense psychological depth in Alceste and elusive subtlety in Célimène.

Alceste

His social standing is self-evident. Unlike the *bons bourgeois* who form the staple butts of Molière's domestic comedies, he is an *homme de qualité*. Oronte, whom no-one would accuse of underestimating his own importance, regards him as an equal. Arsinoé, like Oronte, considers him fitted to the Court. Alceste's costume also marks him out as an *homme de qualité*. Apart from the much-disputed 'rubans verts' (see **46**), Molière seems to have envisaged him in aristocratic dress of the highest fashion and outstanding richness. The costume described in the wardrobe inventory drawn up after Molière's death includes breeches and *justaucorps* (a fitted knee-length coat) of gold-striped brocade and grey silk. It was only between 1665 and 1670 that the *justaucorps* emerged as the the elitist item of Court dress. Alceste's appearance must have visibly undermined his professed loathing for everything to do with the Court. Ironically, he is perfectly suited to his social milieu, in everything except temperament.

It is important to distinguish between Alceste's ideas and his bilious temperament. Molière originally called the play *Le Misanthrope ou l'atrabilaire amoureux*. Although the subtitle had gone when the first edition appeared, the text itself makes great play of the fact that Alceste's fundamental condition is *atrabilaire*. The theory of humours (phlegm, blood, choler or bile, and melancholy) was of immense importance in seventeenth-century physiology for the understanding of an individual's temperament and physical condition. Of the four cardinal humours, melancholy (also called black bile) was the most serious disorder, and was considered to border on madness. Next in order of seriousness came yellow bile, responsible for anger, and which appears to be Alceste's permanent condition. His state is described as 'bile' (90, 166, 449), 'humeur' (1082), 'humeur noire' (91), 'maladie' (105). Repeated references to his 'chagrin' and 'courroux' reinforce the impression of a disturbed temperament. One must assume, then, that when Philinte states 'Mon phlegme est philosophe autant que votre bile' (166), this is not merely a metaphorical manner of speaking but an indication that in contemporary eyes Alceste's distemper is a physiological condition.

There is no intrinsic necessity for Alceste to be in love, other than the fact that it serves Molière's comic purpose. Indeed, reason would seem to preclude the possibility of his loving any woman, let alone a consummate coquette. Alceste is as conscious of this as anyone. But if his love is not psychologically *necessary,* it is amply *justified* by the simple and irrefutable statement that 'la raison n'est pas ce qui règle l'amour' (248).

Célimène

If Tartuffe is the definitive hypocrite and Harpagon the definitive miser, Célimène is the definitive coquette. She is the perfect product of her environment, embodying to the highest degree the elegance, frivolity, cruelty, irony and wit of a highly sophisticated but shallow society. Her beauty, though it is never mentioned in the text, has to be inferred as one of her major assets.

Apart from her personal qualities, Célimène's youth and her status as a widow are crucial for an understanding of the role. We do not know how she comes to be a widow at the age of twenty, though we are allowed to imagine that her independence has been bought at the cost of a marriage of convenience at an early age. At any rate, she is allowed to lead an autonomous existence—a highly desirable condition in an age when young women passed straight from dependency on a father to dependency on a husband. This may not excuse all that she does, but it makes her determination to enjoy herself while she can understandable.

It is worth noting that while Célimène is one of Molière's most memorable creations, her role is actually quite small. She is absent thoughout the first act and most of the last, and speaks only 320 lines out of the total of over 1800. Her major contributions are in the salon scene in Act II, where she outshines everyone, and in the scene of female rivalry in Act III where she wipes the floor with Arsinoé. In the two quarrels with Alceste it is the latter who dominates, while Célimène herself is a rather laconic catalyst. If she makes an impact out of all proportion to the size of her role, this is partly because of the fascination she exerts on the other characters, and partly sustained by the enigma as to her real nature. Much ink has been spilled over the question of Célimène's 'guilt' (does she systematically deceive her suitors? is there any 'truth' in Arsinoé's scandalous insinuations?) and the question of her 'real' feelings (does she 'love' Alceste? does she feel genuine remorse at the end?). But the point is that these questions are unanswerable, and that is part of the mesmeric fascination of the role. In limiting her appearances, Molière must have sensed that the character could not be developed in depth because its very essence is superficiality. Instead, she presents an endlessly smooth exterior. If we could succeed in penetrating the surface, the illusion would probably dissolve into a very banal reality.

Philinte

Since the eighteenth century Philinte has tended to have an unfavourable reception, particularly, as we have already seen, in comparison with the increasingly heroic perception of Alceste's role. To which one responds that critics are entitled to their views, but *il est inutile de chercher midi à quatorze heures*. In polite society of the seventeenth century, Philinte's urbanity, far from being considered a vice, was an essential attribute of courtly behaviour. In Faret's *L'Art de plaire* (1630), under the entry 'De la Complaisance', we read: 'Cette souplesse est l'un des souverains principes de Notre Art, quiconque sait complaire, peut hardiment espérer plaire.' We should note, too, de Visé's evident approval of Philinte: 'L'ami du Misanthrope est si raisonnable que tout le monde devrait l'imiter: il n'est ni trop ni trop peu critique; et ne portant les choses dans l'un ni dans l'autre excès, sa conduite doit être approuvée de tout le monde' (**1**, p. 441).

Arsinoé

The similarity of the *fausse prude* to Tartuffe the *faux dévot* has often been commented on. Both characters wear a mask of virtue to conceal their ruthless self-interest, but Arsinoé is embittered and vindictive into the bargain. In a comedy devoted to variations on the theme of insincerity, Arsinoé occupies a special place. The combination of hypocrisy, gnawing jealousy and false prudery is a particularly deadly one in Molière's eyes. It may have been identified in his mind with the prudes who had attacked *L'École des femmes* for its alleged obscenity. A younger version of the same type can be seen in Armande in *Les Femmes savantes*. Neither Arsinoé nor Armande is a popular role with French actresses, understandably enough, since Molière gives the character-type no compensatory qualities to offset its unpleasantness.

By tradition Arsinoé has tended to be cast as a superannuated matron, an interpretation which finds some support in Célimène's jibe about her ludicrous make-up (942). However, other interpretations are feasible, and perhaps even desirable. In 1666 she was played by Mlle de Brie, an actress who excelled in the role of *jeune première* (Agnès in *L'École des femmes,* Mariane in *Tartuffe,* etc.) and then aged thirty-six. The Parfaict brothers wrote of her that she was 'grande, bien faite, et extrêmement jolie; et la nature lui accorda le don de paraître toujours avec un air de jeunesse' (**27**, p. 13). The text does not tell us how old Arsinoé is, but the question is an important one for the tone of her role and for her relationship with other characters. It is hard to reconcile the idea of a possible match with Alceste if she is a frumpish maid. It is also important to bear her age in mind when we look at the quarrel with Célimène in III, 4.

Éliante

Of the three female characters Éliante makes least impact. That is inevitable and necessary, since her role is to provide a contrast. Less brilliant than Célimène, less highly coloured than Arsinoé, she can appear featureless. She does, however, possess a clearly defined set of qualities and attitudes—sincerity, perceptiveness, tolerance, loyalty. In short, she represents seventeenth-century *honnêteté* at its best. It is intrinsic to the code of *honnêteté* that these qualities are understated. The role is also necessary as a complement to Philinte the *honnête homme* and to provide the obligatory marriage to conclude the comedy. Éliante also contributes a further nuance to our perception of the central character. Even more than Philinte, she casts a sypathetic light on Alceste with her almost unqualified admiration of him. (For a full and extremely sympathetic study of her character and role see **56**).

Clitandre and Acaste

After *Les Précieuses ridicules* no comedy of manners was complete without the *petit marquis,* a conventional type which Molière enjoyed satirising and of which he said: 'Le marquis aujourd'hui est le plaisant de la comédie, et comme dans toutes les comédies anciennes on voit toujours un valet bouffon qui fait rire les auditeurs, de même, dans toutes nos pièces de maintenant, il faut toujours un marquis ridicule qui divertisse la compagnie' (*L'Impromptu de Versailles,* sc. 1). In *Le Misanthrope* he multiplies the enjoyment by giving us two. Like Tweedledum and Tweedledee, they never appear on stage other than as a pair. Their characters, not developed in any depth, are simply resumed: vain, empty-headed, narcissistic. A falsetto voice was a standard feature of the role. The distinguishing trait of the *petit marquis* is an obsession with fashion: in the arts, *précieux* language, and above all in dress. Alceste's 'portrait' of Clitandre (479-86) evokes the ultra-stylish costume of a Court fop of the 1660s: blond wig, vast *rhingrave* (wide breeches resembling a skirt) with big *canons* (lacy knee decoration), a profusion of ribbons, and the curious detail of the 'ongle long qu'il porte au petit doigt' (possibly because it was a fashionable affectation to scratch at doors rather than knock).

Oronte

Completing the trio of male courtiers is a man belonging to a recognisable sub-species: the aristocrat who dabbles in poetry, and whose noble birth gives him an inflated opinion of his artistic merit. (The point is neatly made by Mascarille, the pseudo-marquis in *Les Précieuses ridicules,* when he claims that: 'les gens de qualité savent tout sans avoir jamais rien appris'). It is natural to picture Oronte as being somewhat older than Acaste and Clitandre. Molière treats him more harshly than the latter. Whereas the two *marquis* are people of little consequence, Oronte is a person of some substance and, as events prove, a dangerous enemy. Although a taste for writing could be a harmless eccentricity, in Oronte it is combined with real vindictiveness—probably for reasons of plot rather than from any necessity of character.

Commentary

Act One

Setting

The play is set in Paris. In conformity with the classical unity of place, all the action takes place in a single room in Célimène's house, where she lives with her cousin Éliante. Arnavon argues that the single location is illogical and advocates staging the play with multiple settings (**19**, pp. 184-93). This seems to me to be a distraction which diminishes the play's clarity of focus. The setting is not a nondescript or even a neutral location. It is significant, firstly, from the point of view of *realism*. Molière's stated aim of 'faire reconnaître les gens de votre siècle' implies not only realism in the depiction of contemporary social types but also some topographical realism. The salon—which in a private *hôtel* was more a public place than a domestic retreat—is the natural environment in which to find and observe the fauna of high society. Secondly, the location has a *symbolic* value, representing on a microcosmic scale the wider social milieu which is the play's subject. Finally, it has a *dramatic* importance. The salon of a popular society beauty is a place which naturally gives rise to a much coming and going, and this has a crucial influence on the action. Indeed, it is no exaggeration to say the entire play—not merely the shape of the action but the psychological and emotional action too—is governed by a succession of arrivals and departures.

Scene 1

Molière has often been praised for the quality of his expositions. Those of *Le Misanthrope* and *Tartuffe* are perhaps the finest. At its simplest, the exposition of a play is concerned with conveying the pre-history which the spectator needs in order understand the action. This includes information about characters and about previous events. With

Molière, the former is generally more important than the latter, since his comic formula depends heavily on the presence of a character, and a set of attitudes embodied in a character, as opposed to depending, say, on the convoluted plots of comedies of 'intrigue'. Classical theorists devised a set of prescriptions governing the exposition. It was considered desirable, for example, for the exposition to be contained as far as possible within the first act, as Molière does in this play. Beyond these simple technical requirements, the playwright's aim, ideally, is to make the conveying of information imperceptible, to make it appear as part of the action itself. Molière achieves this in *Le Misanthrope* by presenting Alceste in a towering rage. (This is a classic example of Molière the playwright writing to exploit his own talents as actor. Comic rage was one of his celebrated specialities). The result is that (1) what is essentially a debate becomes an argument, and hence dramatically exciting; (2) the central character is established forcefully and unambiguously from the opening moment; and (3) the spectator's curiosity is aroused as to the cause of Alceste's anger. These are the *theatrical* effects of presenting Alceste in a temper; a further consequence, important where our *interpretation* of what we see is concerned, is that he is shown from the start in a comic, and hence unflattering, light.

What the opening moment presents us with is not an individual but a relationship, in which the whole idea of the play is prefigured. It begins with a physical movement which is both dramatic and symbolic. Alceste's irruption on to the stage, trying to shake Philinte off, not only stamps him with the essential character of an *atrabilaire,* it symbolises his unsociability and also anticipates his final flight from society at the end of the play

Far from presenting the two characters impartially, the opening picture immediately invites the spectator to take sides. Whatever the provocation, Alceste's anger is an unpardonable social solecism. (The entry under 'colère' in Furetière's dictionary (1690) notes that 'C'est une vertu aux hommes de scavoir arrêter les transports de leur colère', and adds bluntly: 'c'est la brutalité des animaux qui les fait suivre les mouvements de leur colère'). His loss of control calls for criticism, and that criticism comes in the form of laughter. Molière instinctively places Alceste's anger in a comic perspective by highlighting the petulant aspect of the tantrum: 'Moi, je veux me fâcher' (5). Philinte's use of the word 'bizarrerie' to characterise Alceste, as early as the second line of the play, is another important signal that we are dealing with someone who is neither mad nor bad but decidedly singular. That impression is confirmed when we learn the reason for Alceste's rage, which is that Philinte has been effusively courteous to someone whom he hardly knows (17-24). Such behaviour is neither more nor less than the common currency of social life. Spectators of any century must be well aware that it is meaningless—not so much a deceit as a harmonising code of behaviour which enables individuals to conduct a collective life. It is this that Alceste claims constitutes a hanging matter (27-8). The disproportion between cause and effect produces a collapse into bathos. Within minutes of his first appearance, Alceste has already been subjected to the first of the comic deflations which are one of the hallmarks of his role.

Having got the play off to a flying start, Molière milks the comic effect briefly with some gentle teasing by Philinte (29-32) which reveals another aspect of Alceste's character—he has no sense of humour—before settling down to a more extended discussion: 'Mais, *sérieusement,* que voulez-vous qu'on fasse?' (34: my italics).The discussion begins with a statement of principle:

> Je veux qu'on soit sincère, et qu'en homme d'honneur,
> On ne lâche aucun mot qui ne parte du cœur. (35-6)

On the face of it this might seem an admirable ideal. It is, however, an abstraction. It is the role of the theatre to translate abstractions into action. Much of the ensuing action will have as its purpose to test the soundness of that abstraction against reality. It will shortly be put concretely to the test with the arrival of Oronte. For the moment we are witnessing a simple discussion. Philinte's objections that common courtesy dictates a measure of conformism to social manners (37-40 & 65-6), allow Alceste to elaborate on his ideas and to give further confirmation of his strange dogmatism. Both his replies begin with an emphatic 'Non', demonstrating how insulated he is from common sense. We also begin to glimpse the complex and less than idealistic motivation that lies behind his rejection of hollow flattery:

> Je refuse d'un cœur la vaste complaisance
> Qui ne fait de mérite aucune différence;
> Je veux qu'on me distingue... (61-3)

Alceste certainly desires to be praised for his exceptional

qualities, but he wants the praise to be sincere, and to be reserved for him alone.

Up to this point (line 76) the debate has been conducted on an abstract level. In theory, Alceste's refusal to recognise a distinction between tact and hypocrisy might be considered praiseworthy, a cult of absolute virtue unsullied by compromise. However, it is when Philinte challenges him with some test cases that we become fully aware of both the real impossibility and the comic potential of Alceste's 'admirable' stance. He enquires whether Alceste is prepared to break it to the aged Émilie that her pathetic make-up makes her a laughing stock, or whether he would tell Dorilas to his face how tiresome his boasting is (81-7). By evoking these miniature dramas the conversation is already starting to suggest the large-scale drama which will result if Alceste applies his principles in practice. His dogmatic responses lead one to fear the worst. Philinte's reply, 'Vous vous moquez' again places Alceste's intransigence in a comic perspective, and simultaneously serves to provoke the latter to yet more extravagant declamations:

> Je ne me moque point,
> Et je vais n'épargner personne sur ce point.
> Mes yeux sont trop blessés, et la cour et la ville
> Ne m'offrent rien qu'objets à m'échauffer la bile.
> J'entre en une humeur noire, en un chagrin profond,
> Quand je vois vivre entre eux les hommes comme ils font. (87-92)

Notice how, in the last four lines above, he tries to rationalize the bilious temperament that controls him. Notice, too, in the ensuing couplet, how the emotion takes control of him and propels him towards ever more excessive language:

> Je ne trouve partout que lâche flatterie,
> Qu'injustice, intérêt, trahison, fourberie; (93-4)

As a result, by the time he declares his mission, it is already invalidated by the irrational anger that has led to it:

> Je n'y puis tenir, j'enrage, et mon dessein
> Est de rompre en visière à tout le genre humain. (95-6)

Philinte's response to this alarmingly uncontrolled display of passion is totally unambiguous: he laughs heartily (98). His comparison of Alceste to the irascible Sganarelle in *L'École des maris* completes the puncturing process. Alceste's humourless reply —'Mon Dieu! laissons là vos comparaisons fades' (101)—anticipates the high-minded disapproval of frivolity which will bring him into conflict with Oronte.

Molière now engages Philinte in longer and more reasoned arguments in favour of (a) making allowance for human nature (146-9, 155, 173-8); (b) moderation (115-6, 151-2); (c) living with the times (117, 145, 153-6); and (d) recognising the futility of trying to change the world (103, 157-8). These are all serious arguments which can only command the spectator's approval. But the scene is not simple polemic. It is a masterly blend of serious discussion, dramatic tension caused by Alceste's emotional response, and gentle comic effect. Philinte delivers another warning to Alceste that he risks making himself into a laughing stock:

> Je vous dirai tout franc que cette maladie,
> Partout où vous allez, donne la comédie,
> Et qu'un si grand courroux contre les moeurs du temps
> Vous tourne en ridicule auprès de bien des gens. (105-108)

It is important to realise that what is being pilloried is not the principles he advances but his 'maladie' and 'courroux', in other words his irrationality. The effect of all Philinte's interventions, mocking and reasoning alike, is a progressive heightening of Alceste's emotional state. This time it does not manifest itself in a climactic tirade. Instead Alceste listens to Philinte with mounting irritation until his patience snaps:

> Je me verrai trahir, mettre en pièces, voler
> Sans que je sois... Morbleu! je ne veux point parler,
> Tant ce raisonnement est plein d'impertinence. (179-81)

The pause and resulting change of tempo allow another shift of focus. With the spectators having been drawn into the play via the moral theme, the exposition proper (i.e. some facts) can now be slipped unobtrusively into place. We learn about the impending lawsuit. Its relevance will not become apparent until much later, when it rebounds inopportunely on Alceste (IV, 4) and helps to precipitate (V, 1) his final break with society. For the moment, it permits the limits of Alceste's principles to be explored further in relation to another test case. Not that Alceste is the only target of satire here. Presumably we are not expected to approve of the judicial practices that are being evoked, and one senses that in an ideal world Alceste would be right to object to them. The point at issue, however, is not whether they are defensible but what, in the world as it is, constitutes a sensible response to them.

Alceste's response, which can be crudely characterised as cutting off his nose to spite his own face, is fatally flawed. Indeed, it calls into question the very basis of his crusade against insincerity. Rather than presenting it as a matter of principle, he positively relishes the prospect of losing his lawsuit because it will justify his hatred of mankind (197-200). To underline the point, Philinte issues a fourth warning:

> On se rirait de vous, Alceste, tout de bon,
> Si l'on vous entendait parler de la façon. (203-204)

The puerile but unanswerable rejoinder—'Tant pis pour qui rirait'—makes further discussion futile.

The resulting short pause allows Philinte to steer the conversation to the question of love, which is the final major dimension of the character and the play. He expresses surprise that someone who has declared war on the human race could be in love (209-12) and, even more improbably, be in love with a woman who is the epitome of everything he detests (213-4 & 217-20), enquiring whether Alceste is blind to her faults (223-4). Philinte's role in this is again to serve as an agent of Alceste's self-revelation, but it is significant that instead of teasing his friend as before, his tone now is one of genuine interest and concern. This alerts the audience to the fact that we are now moving from minor irritants to something potentially more serious. Nevertheless, one cannot help but be struck by the magnificent incongruity of Alceste's predicament, a reaction which Philinte helps to coalesce by his expressions of surprise ('Je m'étonne'; 'ce qui me surprend davantage'; 'd'où vient que'). The key features of Alceste's love for Célimène are briefly established: a hyper-acute awareness of her unworthiness (225-8); an inability, nonetheless, to resist her attractions (229-32); a totally unfounded faith that his love has the power to redeem her (233-4); absolute confidence that Célimène also loves him (235-7); a selfish desire for total possession (240); and lucidity as to the contradictory position he is in (247). It is a complex and unconventional idea of love, and one whose explosive consequences are writ large even at this distance. But given the undeniable premiss that love is irrational, and given Alceste's general attitude to humanity, it is more than psychologically plausible. It must be the *only* form that love can take in a misanthropist.

Further expository lines lay the foundation of the action. Alceste explains:

> Et je ne viens ici qu'à dessein de lui dire
> Tout ce que là-dessus ma passion m'inspire. (241-2)

These words have a double purpose. As well as conveying straightforward information, they whet our appetite for the curious amorous encounter that is to take place. We also learn that 'la sincère Éliante' and 'la prude Arsinoé' both love Alceste, information which not only prepares for the intrigue but also helps to establish a general framework for our understanding of Alceste's character. It places him in the company of a whole gallery of Moliéresque eccentrics who are not fundamentally bad but whose outlook is hugely dominated by a single obsession. Molière himself wrote in connection with Arnolphe in *L'École des femmes:* 'Il n'est pas incompatible qu'une personne soit ridicule en de certaines choses et honnête homme en d'autres' (*La Critique de L'École des femmes,* sc. 6). The fact that at least two women, and quite possibly three, as well as Philinte himself, all feel affection for him is confirmation that except for his *manie,* and indeed in spite of it, he is basically an attractive and even admirable man.

As the scene draws to an end, Philinte issues yet another warning. This time it hints not at impending ridicule but emotional disaster: 'Je crains fort pour vos feux' (249). Molière does not end the scene by resolving the discussion—naturally enough, because what we have witnessed is a *dialogue de sourds*. Instead he brings it to a crashing halt with Oronte's irruption on to the stage.

The essential exposition is now complete. Looking back over the first scene, we are in possession of all the data —social and moral themes, characterisation, and the material for a dramatic action—which the play will develop. A psychological causality has been established which will give everything that follows a sense of inevitability. No plot has yet been engaged, but the dénouement has already been anticipated:

> Et parfois il me prend des mouvements soudains
> De fuir dans un désert l'approche des humains. (143-4)

Scene 2

The first scene has postulated a character, and an attitude to the world, in relation to a social milieu. In exploring aspects of the character and his ideas, Molière has prepared the spectators' responses, and set up expectations. In the ensuing scene those expectations are richly fulfilled. Alceste has adopted an impossibly dogmatic stance which allows him no room for manoeuvre. If he persists in being inflexible, he will be in comic contradiction with the world. If he wavers, he will be in comic self-contradiction. In the second scene we see him do both in turn.

Up to this point Alceste has been countered by a reasoning voice. Now he suddenly finds himself confronting the living embodiment of the cause of his bile, in the person of Oronte. The result is that both dramatically and comically the action shifts to a higher gear. The *scène du sonnet,* although celebrated in its own right, is also important in triggering an intrigue, for the play has reached a point where a plot is needed to give it forward momentum. The quarrel with Oronte will provide a mechanism and a motivation for subsequent action.

In theatre, a character's first appearance is crucial. Oronte's opening statement gives the impression of a monstrous ego bursting upon the stage. What the spectator sees is a man whose dress, manners and self-assurance declare him to be an *homme de qualité*. But it is a comically distorted version of an *homme de qualité*. Oronte's greetings, even by the standards of the day, are excessive, and one only has to read his speech aloud to realise that its swelling rhythms invite the actor to turn the portrayal to caricature with orotund pomposity and accompanying gestures.

The expectations set up by the previous scene ensure, of course, that the spectator's attention is also on Alceste's reaction. His failure to register that Oronte's greeting is addressed to him is a refinement of a traditional *lazzo* (gag) in the *commedia dell'arte* style. After puncturing Oronte's self-importance with this gag, Molière exploits the situation further with more unstoppable effusions (265-76), then develops it into a comedy of misunderstanding when Oronte (1) endorses Alceste's general statement of principle concerning friendship (285-87); (2) offers Alceste what he least desires, advancement at Court (289-92); (3) betrays the real reason for his flattery—he wants to be flattered himself (294-7); and (4) fails fatally to understand that Alceste really means it when he says he will give his honest opinion of the poem (301-304).

These preliminary exchanges (which also have the purpose

of setting up the episode of the sonnet) give us our first glimpse of the comedy of manners in action. It centres on the caricature of an overblown *homme de qualité*. However, we also given a foretaste of Alceste's embarrassment when called upon to put his principles into practice. Oronte not only draws attention to the compliments he has addressed to Alceste, he even hands him an opportunity to repudiate them:

ORONTE C'est à vous, s'il vous plaît, que ce discours s'adresse.

ALCESTE A moi, Monsieur?

ORONTE A vous. Trouvez-vous qu'il vous blesse? (261-2)

Everything that Alceste has said in the previous scene leads us to expect a censorious outburst. What we hear, instead, is a hypocritically polite evasion worthy of the most socialised *homme de cour:*

> Non pas; mais la surprise est fort grande pour moi,
> Et je n'attendais pas l'honneur que je reçoi. (263-4)

The famous *scène du sonnet* proper, which begins at line 305, is developed in four distinct stages: the reading of the poem, Alceste's initial prevarication, the comic catharsis, and the sequel. These should, of course, be indistinguishable to the spectator, but analysis of them will show how Molière works towards the desired end (a quarrel) and the varied forms of satisfaction that are offered to the spectator along the way.

1) Oronte's reading of the poem (305-38), This is prefaced by a series of comic hesitations (a parody of a big build-up), punctuated by Philinte's compliments and Alceste's censorious asides, and rounded off by more of the same. The sonnet itself might legitimately be described as pretentious, but it need not be assumed that Molière was making fun of it *per se*. With its precious sentiment and rhetorical figures, it is a fashionable piece of the period. De Visé says 'le sonnet n'est point méchant, selon la manière d'écrire d'aujourd'hui' (**1**, p. 433). He also reports that during the first performance some spectators applauded the sonnet, only to be 'confus' when Alceste proceeded to condemn it. Later writers have embroidered on the story, claiming that the spectators' resentment at having their good taste challenged contributed to the play's poor reception. La Serre, on dubious authority, claims: 'Le public confus d'avoir pris le change s'indisposa

contre la pièce' (**21**, p. 87). The implication is that the playwright, for once, misjudged his audience. A more likely explanation is that Molière was happy to lead those spectators who fell for it into a trap. There can be little doubt that whatever the sonnet's intrinsic merits, Oronte's fatuous delivery of it is intended to produce a comic effect.

Why, then, is Philinte so fulsome in his praise? If we discount the unlikely hypothesis that he really does consider the sonnet a masterpiece, we are left with only two possibilities: either he is being hypocritical or he is ironic. Critics who are hostile to Philinte have naturally seen his praise of the sonnet as abject flattery. Others, for whom Philinte is a conduit for common sense, see him to be taunting Alceste. Michaut, on the other hand, suggests he is trying to defuse a dangerous situation by massaging Oronte's vanity, and loyally protecting his friend, by preventing him from expressing an opinion which he (Philinte) knows will cause trouble (**30**, p. 229). This view might conceivably be justified by Philinte's explanation in the next scene: 'j'ai bien vu qu'Oronte, afin d'être flatté...' (441). The scene on its own, though, cannot provide an answer. The interpretation most consistent with the ironic detachment Philinte exhibits on other occasions would be that he is enjoying the spectacle of two people making fools of themselves, and contributing to the fun by teasing the one and mocking the vanity of the other. Only later, at the end of the scene when the quarrel takes a dangerous turn, does he intervene to calm things down.

2) Alceste's prevarication (339-75). It is not Philinte's opinion that Oronte really wants, however, and the next stage begins when he turns the heat on Alceste:

> Mais, pour vous, vous savez quel est notre traité:
> Parlez-moi, je vous prie, avec sincérité. (339-40)

It is the first major test of his principles, though we have already been given a foretaste, with his reaction to Oronte's greetings, of a possible outcome. We now have the comedy of the plain dealer's reluctance to speak the truth. It is a marvellously subtle comedy of discomfiture, prolonged by the poet's inability (genuine or feigned?) to grasp the fact that the oblique criticism is directed to him. The obvious irony lies in Alceste's failure, encapsulated in the repeated 'je ne dis pas cela', to live up to the principles he has recently proclaimed with such vigour. There is, however, a further layer of irony in the situation, for in order to avoid plain speaking Alceste adopts a device (reporting his advice to an acquaintance in a similar case) in which he contrives to present himself as a plain speaker, sternly and fearlessly delivering unpalatable truths (343-50). It is pointless to speculate, as some have done, about whether Alceste's reported conversation with an acquaintance is 'real' or fictitious. On the other hand, it is worth asking whether the advice he gives is necessarily invalidated by the situation. The idea that a gentleman-poetaster would be well advised to keep his writings to himself, although intemperately expressed, may well be one which had Molière's approval.

3) The comic catharsis (374-416). This comes when Alceste is finally pinned down by Oronte's dawning understanding:

> Voilà qui va fort bien, et je crois vous entendre.
> Mais ne puis-je savoir ce que dans mon sonnet...? (374-5)

Just as Alceste was comic when he prevaricated, so he is comic when he speaks his mind. The truth, when it comes, emerges like a pent-up force. 'Franchement', he says, 'il est bon à mettre au cabinet' (376). For modern audiences 'cabinet' has acquired a crude comic connotation which was not intended; in the seventeenth century 'cabinet' could mean a study or (the meaning presumably intended here) a bureau-type desk with multiple compartments. The insult to Oronte is still plain enough. What follows—his scornful reading of lines from the sonnet and his critical comments—is all the more offensive to Oronte for being so dismissively offhand: 'ce n'est que jeux de mots, qu'affectation pure' (387). What Alceste objects to is the artificiality of the sonnet. In identifying it (rightly, as we have seen) as a product of the prevailing fashion, he also betrays himself as an enemy of modernity. The idea that Alceste is out of joint with his time was suggested earlier when he objected to 'ces vices du temps' (59) and 'vos gens à la mode' (42; see also Philinte's reply, 153-6).

Warming to his theme, Alceste launches into a double rendition of his own preferred *chanson*. This time there can be no possible ambiguity about where Molière expected his audience to stand: the verse may be pleasant enough, but Philinte's amusement (414) shows that its old-fashioned rusticity make it ridiculous in the eyes of sophisticated society. Alceste's final summation:

> Oui, Monsieur le rieur, malgré vos beaux esprits,
> J'estime plus cela que toute la pompe fleurie
> De tous ces faux brillants, où chacun se récrie. (414-6)

throws down the gauntlet to Oronte and leads automatically to:

4) The sequel (417-38). This short, heated exchange is the natural and inevitable climax of the scene. There is a sudden change of tempo, with a rapid-fire exchange of brief *répliques,* and a change of tone, as the earlier veneer of civility falls away to reveal naked insults. Notice the geometry of these exchanges, giving the clash the quality of a stylised fencing duel. It builds rapidly to a crescendo, is held in suspension by Philinte's belated intervention, and resolved by an indignant exit. The final irony is Alceste, the scourge of insincerity, returning the hollowest and most conventional of polite phrases to the retreating Oronte: 'Et moi, je suis, Monsieur, votre humble serviteur' (438).

Scene 3

Alceste and Philinte remain on stage to survey the damage. In terms of theatrical rhythm this scene provides the necessary *ralentissement* before precipitating us into the next big scene. But it is more than a simple interlude. It is necessary for the characters to take stock of the situation after the quarrel which ended the previous scene, and for Molière to refocus the action. Philinte's opening remark:

> Hé bien! vous le voyez: pour être trop sincère,
> Vous voilà sur les bras une fâcheuse affaire... (439-40)

does both these things. As well as drawing the obvious lesson, it also anticipates the future consequences of the quarrel for the plot. Alceste's restless movement and near-speechless state must have allowed Molière scope for expressive physical playing to comic effect. The act ends as it began, with Alceste trying to shake off a doggedly loyal Philinte, before rebounding on to an unsuspecting Célimène in the next act.

Act Two

Analysis of the act

The centrepiece of the act is the *scène du salon,* which brings a broadening of the social canvas and with it an amplification of the comedy of manners. The act begins, however, with a resumption of the action, i.e. the question of Alceste's quarrel with Célimène. As was made clear in I, 1, this is the business which motivates his presence at her house, and from which the following scene was the first of a succession of distractions. But it has hardly been broached (scene 1) when Alceste is again frustrated, this time by the arrival of the other salon *habitués* (scenes 2 & 3). The comedy of manners, which is the assumed background to the discussion with Philinte, and of which we have had a prior glimpse in the figure of Oronte, now comes to the fore during the long central scene (scene 4). It offers a further living demonstration of the falseness that Alceste condemned in the opening scene. The depiction of aristocratic manners can be enjoyed for itself as satire, but it also draws a violent reaction from Alceste. His reaction is a complex one, combining anger at their backbiting gossip and jealousy at the way in which Célimène enjoys her admirers' flattery. In this way the two aspects of Alceste's character—the *misanthrope* and the *atrabilaire amoureux*—come together, and merge in the comedy of manners. By the end of the scene, therefore, the attention has shifted back to to Alceste. He threatens to provoke the confrontation he has been seeking, before a new distraction intervenes (scenes 5 & 6), as a consequence of his quarrel with Oronte.

At the end of the act Alceste's affair with Célimène stands exactly where it did at the start. That, of course, is the intended point. Molière compensates for the lack of movement by the age-old device of dramatic suspense, using Alceste's frustration to maintain an illusion of dramatic momentum.

Scene 1

Dramatically, the scene has a double purpose: to refocus

the action after the episode with Oronte, and to give us a tantalising foretaste of the big *scène à deux* between Alceste and Célimène in Act Four. It also hints at the eventual outcome of their relationship. Alceste *begins* his attempt to settle matters with Célimène with the prophetic statement: 'Tôt ou tard nous romprons indubitablement' (452). Structurally, the scene completes a sequence of three complementary episodes each of which explores a particular aspect of the general theme of sincerity and hypocrisy. The two earlier scenes have dealt with the effects of Alceste's mania for sincerity, first in relation to politeness, and then in relation to poetry. We are now going to see the same process in relation to love. The general pattern of the scene repeats that of the two previous scenes, and for the same reason: Alceste's choleric temperament makes social intercourse without argument impossible. It therefore begins with Alceste quarrelsome and finishes with him in a temper.

Strictly speaking, there is no continuity of action between this scene and the previous act. Alceste has left the house at the end of Act I, and on his way out met Célimène returning from her shopping expedition (250-1 & 456). The brief absence is important in allowing him to regain some composure after the emotional high at the end of the first act. Without some such prior diminuendo, the quarrel would not be able to build to its own climax.

The scene gives us our first taste of the psychological comedy of love. The two characters interact to produce a subtle comedy of insincerity combined with a highly sophisticated version of the traditional comedy of jealousy. True to type, and with no preamble, the plain-speaking *atrabilaire amoureux* launches straight into a reproach (447-8) before proceeding to enumerate his grounds for jealousy. For the spectator this brusque attack is doubly satisfying. At one level it is a fulfilment of our expectations, because it is so wholly predictable. Alceste has given a clear warning that he will spare Célimène no criticism (225-8). Nevertheless, it must still come as something of a surprise as we register the full incongruity of the lover's behaviour in action, now that he is finally alone with the object of his affection. Célimène's first words characterise her immediately as someone who has extreme poise and piercing irony, the essential qualities which make her the epitome of *la vie mondaine*. She allows him just enough rope to hang himself before responding with a question which adroitly parries the charge and turns the attack back on to him:

> C'est pour me quereller donc, à ce que je voi,
> Que vous avez voulu me ramener chez moi? (455-6)

Within seconds of their meeting, although he does not yet realise it, Alceste is being driven from an attacking position to a defensive one. It is a situation we will see repeated in the *scène des portraits* and again in the second quarrel with Célimène.

Molière proceeds to explore their relationship with great psychological insight. What we are witnessing is not the conventional comic situation of a contrived misunderstanding. It is a collision between two people behaving true to type to the highest degree. For Célimène, love is a game, played with such a light touch that it is impossible for the spectator to judge the real nature of her feelings. Where Alceste is concerned, however, it seems undeniable that we are witnessing a genuine passion of sorts. Their encounter provides a vivid demonstration of the simple but profound truth that people in love behave in accordance with their fundamental nature. The comedy springs from an extreme incompatibility in every significant aspect of their existence: general outlook, conception of love, capacity for feeling, and temperament. Ironically, Alceste complains that it is 'votre humeur, Madame' that is the root of the problem (457).

The scene is a sophisticated reworking of what is, at bottom, a traditional situation of farce: the coquette running rings round a jealous lover. The development which gives it rhythm is a self-defeating loss of control by the offended party. Alceste has come intending to pick a quarrel with Célimène, but his temper has cooled. The first phase of the quarrel, therefore, is marked by an attempt at 'reasonableness' on his part:

> Madame, voulez-vous que je vous parle net?
> De vos façons d'agir je suis mal satisfait. (447-8)

In the scale of Alceste's emotions, this is commendably dispassionate. In fact, the comedy in this initial approach lies precisely in the way that Alceste believes he is behaving reasonably, though in reality his dogmatism will leave him little room for manoeuvre. His second and third speeches, although argumentative, must also seem to him to be conciliatory: 'Je ne querelle point' (457), and 'Non, ce n'est pas, Madame, un bâton qu'il faut prendre' (465). The turning point in the quarrel comes in the middle of the scene, when Célimène concludes:

> Mais de tout l'univers vous devenez jaloux. (495)

and Alceste replies:

> C'est que tout l'univers est bien reçu de vous. (496)

This is a couplet of superb comic limpidity. The two antithetical statements, one detached and ironic, the other impassioned, and both of them true, resume the quintessential difference between the characters. Alceste's reply is like an involuntary *cri de cœur* in which all his jealousy is discharged. It initiates a second phase consisting of a series of shorter *répliques* and building towards a crisis. Célimène's deceptively reasonable answers provoke Alceste into increasingly crass declarations of jealousy (501-502; 504), leading him into a trap of his own making. He himself springs the trap when he finally insinuates that Célimène is deceiving him:

> Mais qui m'assurera que dans le même instant,
> Vous n'en disiez peut-être aux autres tout autant? (507-508)

(Compare with his more general statement to Philinte: 'Je veux qu'on me distingue'). It invites the inevitable reply:

> Certes, pour un amant la fleurette est mignonne,
> Et vous me traitez là de gentille personne.
> Hé bien! pour vous ôter d'un semblable souci,
> De tout ce que j'ai dit je me dédis ici, (509-12)

This coquettish taunt unleashes the climax, a most extravagant demonstration of Alceste's 'bizarrerie' in love:

> Morbleu, faut-il que je vous aime?
> Ah! que si de vos mains je rattrape mon cœur,
> Je bénirai le Ciel de ce rare bonheur! [...]
> Mais mes plus grands efforts n'ont rien fait jusqu'ici,
> Et c'est pour mes péchés que je vous aime ainsi.
> (514-16; 519-20)

We can see very clearly how Alceste's feelings and the logic of the situation have led him to this outburst. And at the same time we are aware of the profound paradox that makes it an impossible way for a man to declare his love. Any residual temptation we might have to side emotionally with Alceste is kept in check by Célimène's irony. First she punctures his self-pity by saying: 'Il est vrai, votre ardeur est pour moi sans seconde' (521).This statement is clearly ironic. Amazingly, Alceste seems too lacking in control to register the irony, for he continues:

> Oui, je puis là-dessus défier tout le monde.
> Mon amour ne se peut concevoir, et jamais
> Personne n'a, Madame, aimé comme je fais. (522-4)

To which her irresistibly witty retort again makes it impossible not to laugh with Célimène against Alceste:

> En effet, la méthode en est toute nouvelle,
> Car vous aimez les gens pour leur faire querelle; (523-6)

Still blind to his own ridicule, Alceste makes one final effort at self-mastery:

> Mais il ne tient qu'à vous que son chagrin ne passe.
> A tous nos démêlés coupons chemin, de grâce,
> Parlons à cœur ouvert, et voyons d'arrêter... (529-31)

before being halted in his tracks by the appearance of Basque.

Scenes 2 and 3

These follow directly on from the previous scene, and build on the tension of Alceste's semi-contained anger. Molière varies and accumulates the comic effect by staging the announcements of the visitors' arrival successively, rather than together. The announcement of Acaste (scene 2) prompts further recriminations from Alceste. Célimène's defence of her decision to receive him permits, in turn, a miniature caricature of the social type (a variety of *médisant*) which he represents. In contrast, news of Clitandre's arrival (scene 3), interrupting Alceste in mid-sentence for the second time, is the last straw. The effect this time is to produces a brief comedy of indecision when Alceste turns on his heels to go, refuses Célimène's appeal for him to stay, then finally remains to sulk. De Visé's account (**1**, p. 435) suggests that in the 1666 production Molière prolonged the comedy with a further false exit after Célimène has given him permission to leave (558).

Scene 4

This is the longest scene in the play and the one which brings most of the main characters together for the first time. It is static, consisting essentially of a seated conversation. But it offers high comedy, a subtle satire of the finest quality. The comic tone is set by the social milieu, one characterised by mesure, sophistication and wit. There are none of the broad comic effects produced by the burlesque 'salon' and ludicrous pseudo-marquis of *Les Précieuses ridicules*. Molière evidently felt that a play depicting genuine high society demanded something more delicate and vraisemblable. The nearest equivalent we have is in *La Critique de l'École des femmes,* a comedy set in an almost identical social environment. As in that play, the scene should give us the impression of witnessing a natural conversation, subtly heightened for satirical effect. The ambiance is relaxed and unforced. For all its obvious falseness it has elegance and a lightness of touch. All these qualities guarantee that Alceste will appear to crash about like a bull in a china shop.

Three new characters are introduced: Acaste, Clitandre and Éliante. Molière has prepared for these arrivals with the scrupulous attention to detail that is a feature of the play. The appearance of the first two has been anticipated in a general way by Alceste's denunciation of Court society in the first scene. More specifically, Clitandre has been characterised in advance by Alceste's portrait of him as an affected coxcomb (476-88), and Acaste by Célimène's portrait of him as an influential Court gossip (542-8). The appearance of 'la sincère Éliante' has also been prepared in I, 1 (215). She speaks so few lines that her role in the scene may seem redundant. In fact, her presence is important for a number of reasons. She serves to double with Philinte in supplying a norm of *honnêteté* to set against the gossipers, on the one hand, and the *atrabilaire* on the other. As well as a general outlook characterised by sincerity, she offers a concept of uncorrupted love to contrast with Alceste's and Célimène's. The alliance that is established between her and Philinte in this scene also prepares for their eventual marriage.

It is not by accident that the characters are introduced in pairs. Éliante enters first, accompanied by Philinte. Their unceremonious entry underlines the informal nature of the gathering. Clitandre appears a few moments later, with Acaste hard on his heels. The duo represent variations on the basic type of self-satisfied courtier. They arrive in time to interrupt Alceste who has profited from the delay to threaten Célimène with the prospect of an ugly scene (561-6).

Clitandre's opening sally:

> Parbleu! je viens du Louvre, où Cléonte, au levé,
> Madame, a bien paru ridicule achevé. (567-8)

is worth considering for the rich dramatic interest that is compacted into it. In two lines tone, character and action are established. The off-hand 'Parbleu' offers an immediate contrast of tone with Alceste's incessant 'morbleu'. The awkward climate caused by the latter's grumpiness is suddenly replaced by one of playfulness. Alceste and his problems are forced into the background. Although he falls silent until his outburst at line 651, he remains visible to the spectator throughout the scene as an incongruous brooding presence. Clitandre's opening words, with the attention-seeking 'parbleu' and 'je viens du Louvre', serve also to mark the character of a vain and empty-headed courtier. In a group of rivals obsessed with nuances of social distinction, his casual reference to his presence at the King's 'levé' is intended to impress everyone with the special privileges he enjoys at Court. The narcissism of the gathering is also demonstrated, for it is clear from his attack on Cléonte that gossip about absent friends is the order of the day. Although there are four people on stage, the parenthetical 'Madame' in his second line tells us that Célimène is the focus of attention. The speech, finally, is a ball tossed into the conversation. As intended, it is caught and deftly returned by Célimène:

> Dans le monde, à vrai dire, il se barbouille fort... (571 ff.)

Whereupon Acaste bowls her another ball:

> Parbleu! s'il faut parler des gens extravagants,
> Je viens d'en essuyer un des plus fatigants... (575-6)

Thus, effortlessly, the *scène des portraits* is engaged.

Portraiture, one of the most demanding manifestations of verbal wit, is a major motif throughout the play. In this scene alone Célimène delivers nine portraits, including one of Alceste, in addition to her earlier sketch of Acaste (542-8). We have already heard two previous sketches with Philinte's evocation of the braggart Dorilas and the decrepit Émilie (81-6). Ironically, Alceste's disapproval of the device does not prevent him resorting to it himself when he gives his uncomplimentary portrait of Clitandre (II, 1). The use of portraits as a theatrical device is both realistic and inspired. Célimène's gallery of social type opens up a new range of targets for Molière's satire. The result is a play which is unique in the way it goes beyond the treatment of individuals to suggest a picture of a whole social class. We are reminded of the braggarts, the bores, the wits and the dimwits, the scandal-mongers—in short, all the parasites of Court society. But portraiture is also a natural device for characterising those who indulge in the pastime. The *scène des portraits* contributes to the impression of a microsociety obsessed with itself. Célimène and her admiring listeners unconsciously betray both the things to which they attach most value (appearances, wit, verbal dexterity) and the mechanisms that govern their relations (rivalry, flattery, malicious gossip). It is entirely fitting that it is Célimène's gift for portraits that is eventually turned against her to produce the dénouement.

Like Hamlet's soliloquies, the portraits have become so familiar with time that it is notoriously difficult to deliver them without giving the impression of reciting set pieces. Properly performed, however, they will give the impression of spontaneous and effortless wit. Molière sustains interest, firstly by varying the length and emphasis of the portraits and the pattern of the repartee, and secondly by imposing on the whole scene a subtle movement towards a crescendo. The character assassination becomes increasingly malicious and, as the scene develops, we see an increasing polarisation among the listeners. Alceste watches disapprovingly from a distance. Acaste and Clitandre encourage Célimène with mounting hilarity. The *honnêtes gens* Philinte and Éliante remain more detached—not necessarily disapproving but not participating in the *médisance* either. As the attacks become more acrimonious, however, Éliante intervenes with her defense of Cléon: 'Il prend soin d'y servir des mets fort délicats' (627). Its effect, however, is to allow Célimène to cap it with a witty riposte: 'Oui, mais je voudrais qu'il ne s'y servît pas.' Philinte's intervention—'On fait assez de cas de son oncle Damis' (631)—is intended in the same spirit as Éliante's, as we see from Célimène's reply, 'Il est de mes amis.' This provides a moment of high theatrical effect. Célimène pauses momentarily for the listeners to register their unease, then audaciously continues: 'mais...' and proceeds to demolish her friend nonethless. The portrait is of a man whose censorious attitude bears some similarity to Alceste's. Indeed, it may be that Alceste is spurred to intervene at this point precisely because he sense the satire is directly obliquely at him. The torrent of compliments from Célimène's admirers now reaches a crescendo:

ACASTE Dieu me damne! voilà son portrait véritable.

CLITANDRE Pour bien peindre les gens vous êtes admirable! (649-50)

and we sense that the conversation has reached some kind of plateau. This supplies the cue for Alceste to step in.

Although Alceste is visibly irritated, his first speech (651-6) is a restrained sneer. This heightens the theatrical effect of his anger when it does explode. The trigger is Clitandre's taunt:

> Pourquoi s'en prendre à nous? Si ce qu'on dit vous blesse,
> Il faut que le reproche à Madame s'adresse. (657-8)

Wittingly or unwittingly, Clitandre's remark touches a raw nerve in Alceste. When alone with Célimène he does not mince his words, as we have just seen. As a lover, however, he hardly wishes to be drawn into criticising her in front of his rivals. Sidestepping the challenge, he discharges his rage on Clitandre and, by implication, Acaste:

> Non, morbleu! c'est à vous; et vos ris complaisants
> Tirent de son esprit tous ces traits médisants. (659-60)

Now that the *scène des portraits* has been brought to a crashing end, Molière's aim is to steer the action back to the central matter of Alceste's quarrel with Célimène. The general movement of the rest of the scene, therefore, which starts with his condemnation of gossip, takes us first from an attack on her admirers to an attack on Célimène herself. From this arises a discussion in which Alceste is obliged to defend his singular concept of love, and which indirectly poses his jealousy as the central problems. This is turn brings the scene back to its starting point and sets the stage for his summons to appear before the *maréchaux*.

In his tirade against malicious gossip we see again how his anger works against him. Alceste may be 'right' to disapprove of their hypocrisy (653-6) and flattery (659-66). At some level the spectators' amusement at the school for scandal will certainly have been mixed with critical disapproval. But the weight of Alceste's criticism is undermined by the excess of his language (he speaks of 'coupable encens' and 'vices') betraying his usual failure to keep a proper sense of perspective. In this respect, it is significant that Philinte and Éliante 'change sides'. After previously distancing themselves from the laughter of Célimène and her admirers, they now line up against Alceste. Philinte's question:

> Mais pourquoi pour ces gens un intérêt si grand,
> Vous qui condamneriez ce qu'en eux on reprend? (667-8)

can be taken as a taunt, or possibly an attempt to bring Alceste back to reason. In either case it has the effect of drawing attention to his isolation. It also supplies the cue for Célimène's last and most telling portrait, that of Alceste himself:

> Et ne faut-il pas bien que Monsieur contredise?
> A la commune voix veut-on qu'il se réduise,
> Et qu'il ne fasse pas éclater en tous lieux
> L'esprit contrariant qu'il a reçu des cieux? (669-72)

Her portrait of Alceste is a brilliant summary of what makes him appear so singular to Célimène's set. It is amusing because, although it is one-sided and distorted, it is devastatingly perceptive as far as it goes. Célimène, understandably, has no sense of the moral crusade on which he is engaged, nor of the depth of feeling of which he is capable. But we are compelled to recognise that the 'esprit contrariant' and the 'soif de distinction', which Alceste revealed so abundantly to Philinte in the first scene, are wittily and accurately described.

Alceste's petulant and ineffectual reply ('Les rieurs sont pour vous, Madame'—a concealed stage direction) shows him again at a loss for an argument. (Compare with 'Tant pis pour qui rirait'—205). Philinte's attempt to defuse the crisis by reasoning with him (683-6) has the contrary effect (687-90). Now, at last, he is unable to restrain himself from reproaching Célimène herself:

> Non, Madame, non: quand j'en devrais mourir,
> Vous avez des plaisirs que je ne puis souffrir;
> Et l'on a tort, ici, de nourrir dans votre âme
> Ce grand attachement aux défauts qu'on y blâme. (691-4)

The first couplet is an impetuous release of what Alceste has been trying to suppress. The second couplet represents a vain attempt to draw back to his original position of pinning the blame on her admirers. We see instantly that the retreat comes too late. Alceste has committed the unpardonable social blunder of criticising the hostess, and the sycophants spring to her defence with laughable transparency (695-8). We register the comedy of their absurd flattery, but the main focus of attention is still Alceste. Having exposed himself, he now has no option but to do what he has been striving to avoid, and presses on with his criticism of Célimène:

> Ils frappent tous la mienne; et loin de m'en cacher,
> Elle sait que j'ai soin de les lui reprocher.
> Plus on aime quelqu'un, moins il faut qu'on le flatte;
> A ne rien pardonner le pur amour éclate; (699-702)

Alceste at least has the merit of being consistent with his principles when he declares that a lover must never flatter or seek to excuse the object of his love. But it takes only a subtle shift of emphasis by Célimène to bring out its absurdity. Her observation that for Alceste 'bien injurier les personnes qu'on aime' is the highest mark of love is but the merest distortion of the truth.

Éliante's homily (translated from Lucretius) is not incongruous in the context of a high society salon, where conversation often dwelt on such abstractions. It serves a thematic purpose in developing an idea of uncorrupted love in contrast to Alceste's tyrannically unforgiving love and the shameless flattery that conventional courtship involves. The speech is actually very charming, though of questionable dramatic interest. It is generally felt to be too long and too artificial for its charm to be appreciated. Alceste apparently has registered nothing of what Éliante says (731), whilst Célimène and the two *marquis* seem to be waiting impatiently for her to finish speaking. Molière uses this to provide Célimène with a cue to bring the scene to an end ('Brisons là ce discours, Et dans la galerie allons faire deux tours', 731-2).

Scene 4 ends with a childish display of jealousy when Alceste again tries to force Célimène to choose between him and his rivals. In a circuitous manner the action has come full circle back to the point at which the scene started. Whereas in scene 3 Alceste was determined to leave, now he is determined to remain, in the hope that he will eventually be left alone with Célimène. But the play has already established the basic mechanism whereby he is to be comically frustrated in that ambition. The appearance of Basque and then of the Garde is a repetition of what has by now become a pattern of interruptions. (Oronte, I, 2, and the salon visitors, II, 2). The essential laughter, the profound irony in this variant, lies in the fact that it arises out of the first interruption and that Alceste has brought it on his own head.

Since an explanation is required of why Alceste has been summoned, Molière can plausibly extract further comedy from Alceste by evoking the original quarrel with Oronte. Philinte's explanation is phrased in a way to set the matter in its proper perspective: it is nothing more than a 'ridicule affaire' (754) involving 'certains petits vers' (756). It is against this perspective that we are invited to contemplate Alceste's determination to treat it as a matter of principle. Unity of place prevents us from being shown Alceste's appearance before the *maréchaux,* but we can savour it at a distance when he declares that he will stand by his opinion of the sonnet. Reacting predictably to Philinte's appeal for moderation, he talks himself into a frenzy of obstinacy by way of a series of increasingly vehement declarations: 'je n'aurai jamais de lâche complaisance'; 'Je ne me dédis point'; 'Je n'en démordrai point'; 'rien n'aura pouvoir / De me faire dédire'. The familiar pattern of mounting indignation builds to a strident climax, and the laughter it causes among the listeners provokes the inevitable comic descent:

> Hors qu'un commandement exprès du Roi me vienne
> De trouver bons les vers dont on se met en peine,
> Je soutiendrai toujours, morbleu! qu'ils sont mauvais,
> Et qu'un homme est pendable après les avoir faits.
> *(A Clitandre et à Acaste qui rient.)*
> Par le sangbleu! Messieurs, je ne croyais pas être
> Si plaisant que je suis. (769-74)

According to Boileau, Molière delivered the last words with a bitter laugh which delighted the spectators (**1**, p. 494).

Alceste's exit lines, in which he promises to resume his quarrel with Célimène at the earliest possible moment, end the act on a note of suspense.

Act Three

Analysis of the act

By now the main characters and themes are firmly established, and an action has been engaged. The third act, as is commonly the case, can therefore afford to leave the intrigue in suspension and develop subsidiary complications. This is also the natural point at which to introduce the last significant character, Arsinoé. With Alceste temporarily removed from the action, the focus is on rivalries involving secondary characters: Clitandre and Acaste conclude a competitive pact (scene 1), then Arsinoé comes to declare open war on Célimène (scene 4). These two scenes seem at the time to be simply an extension of the tableau of society life, yet they will both prove to be very relevant to the Alceste-Célimène affair, though in a way that is not at first apparent.

Arsinoé's arrival seems like the chance product of the ebb and flow of salon life. In fact, it is not a casual social call. She has come for a precise reason, which is obviously not the one she offers to Célimène (concern for her friend's reputation), nor yet the one which the audience quickly discerns behind her hypocritically friendly advice (to score points off her rival). Armed with the letter which, we discover much later (lines 1336-40) has been to given to her by Oronte, and exulting in the prospect of confounding her rival, she has come with the purpose of snatching Alceste for herself, which is what she proceeds to attempt in scene 5. If the ploy fails, the letter will at least allow her the consolation of extracting revenge on both Alceste and Célimène. Indirectly, all this is a further product of Alceste's encounter with Oronte in the first act. Although there is no mention of Oronte by name in this act, we discover later that he is behind Arsinoé's manoeuvre. The two have joined forces in an alliance to destroy their respective enemies. Alternatively, Arsinoé believes she is profiting from Oronte's indiscretion for her own advantage, while in fact she is a pawn manipulated by Oronte in his own vendetta against Alceste. We are not told, neither do we need to know, which of these version is 'true'. Either way, threads are being drawn together which will eventually converge in the final act.

Of course, neither Arsinoé nor Oronte achieves the revenge she seeks. At the last minute, it turns to humiliation for both of them. Nor are they finally the architects of the *dénouement:* that role falls to the two *marquis,* in a development which is a consequence of the first scene of the act.

Scene 1

Left to occupy the stage, Acaste and Clitandre enact a characteristic comedy of vanity. The former's self-satisfied preening is perfectly complemented by the latter's smugness In terms of dramatic rhythm, this extremely amusing scene provides a relaxed interlude between the débâcle at the end of the previous act and the high drama of the next scene. Thematically, it extends the range of Molière's depiction of various types of love, a facet of the human comedy in which every character in the play is involved. For the two narcissistic *soupirants,* love is simply an extension of their vanity. The scene particularly invites comparison with the ensuing cat-fight, another encounter where amorous rivalry is conducted under a veneer of social refinement. The ultimate purpose of their meeting, however, is to prepare the dénouement, which springs from their agreement to show each other any proof which either might receive of Célimène's favours. For the moment, the two men's self-confidence augments suspicions about her multiple infidelities but without offering any conclusive evidence.

Scenes 2 & 3

Célimène rejoins the visitors and Arsinoé is announced. Her role in the action has been formally prepared in the exposition by references to her prudery and her feelings for Alceste (216). Repeating the device employed in II, 2-3, Molière uses the *scènes de liaison* to demolish the character in advance by means of another of Célimène's satirical *portraits.* In a few incisive brush strokes we are given the essential Arsinoé: she is a hypocrite (853-5) whose failure to attract men (855-6) has made her frustrated (862), envious (857-8), embittered (860) and a pseudo-prude (861), though her secret ambition is still to have a lover (865). Of more direct relevance to the plot, we also learn that she hopes to win Alceste (866), and in her jealousy (867-8) is waging an underhand campaign to discredit Célimène (869-70). The portrait leads us to expect a particularly odious character, and we are amply gratified when Arsinoé appears.

Scene 4

The scene between Célimène and Arsinoé is the definitive comic portrayal of female rivalry. It is a fencing bout played with the apparently bated foils of an elaborate social code, but with deadly serious malicious intent. It ends with a defiant challenge to compete for lovers, offering an intriguing parallel to the good-humoured pact agreed by the Clitandre and Acaste in the previous scene.

In keeping with the play's prevailing tone of *vraisemblance,* the fight is not noticeably stylised. However, if we look below the surface at its structure and rhythms, we can see that it is artfully contrived to extract the maximum dramatic effect. The preliminaries are reduced to a perfunctory minimum, and the fight is in three rounds: (1) a symmetrical pair of long speeches in which each woman mounts an assault on her adversary's general conduct; this is equivalent to opening battle with canons and heavy artillery; (2) a stand-off, leading to a short skirmish in which Célimène taunts Arsinoé about her age; (3) another stand-off, then a no-holds-barred fight to the death on the real issue, rivalry over men.

The preliminaries start on a note of high comedy with Célimène's sudden switch of behavioural mask when Arsinoé makes her entrance:

> Enfin je n'ai rien vu de si sot à mon gré,
> Elle est impertinente au suprème degré,
> Et ...
>   Ah! quel heureux sort en ce lieu vous amène?
> Madame, sans mentir, j'étais de vous en peine. (871-4)

The device is an exaggerated variation on her hypocritical reception of Acaste after painting him in uncomplimentary terms (II, 4). Notice the audacious 'sans mentir' in the last line. The expression falls readily from the lips of everyone in the play. Often it is comic because it is unconscious. I suggest that the comic effect is greater here if Célimène uses it knowingly. Her effusive greeting of Arsinoé represents comic insincerity of a particular kind: it is not a self-interested mask of hypocrisy, nor is it even meant to deceive. She neither wants nor expects to obtain anything from Arsinoé, but is amusing herself at the expense of her rival with a daringly exaggerated display of insincerity. Clitandre and Acaste, who remain on stage until line 876, supply the indispensable audience. Dispensing with the usual formulas of politeness, Arsinoé tries to come straight to the point (875), is impatient for the other visitors to leave (877), and declines the offer of a chair (878). The effect is to suggest a strained atmosphere in marked contrast to the casual elegance of the earlier salon scene. Arsinoé then fires the opening salvo.

Under the guise of proffering friendly advice and of reporting what enemies have said about her, she delivers a comprehensive condemnation of the coquette's way of life. Molière ensures that on this occasion our sympathies lie entirely with Célimène. The fact that Arsinoé has arrived uninvited to deliver gratuitous insults places her in an unfavourable light. In contrast to Célimène's playful insincerity, her hypocrisy is a cover for spiteful malice. The nature of her attack further defines her character. As a prude she fixes on the scandalous appearance of Célimène's behaviour, but proceeds by insinuation ('votre galanterie'; 'l'air dont vous viviez'; 'tous vos déportements') to imply the worst. In her first long speech one can distinguish at least four aspects to the hypocrite's mask: protestations of friendship (879-80; 884), feigned concern for Célimène's reputation (881-3; 893-4), alleged concern for her spiritual welfare (895-6), the transparent fiction of merely reporting what others have said. The mask is all the more repellent for the way it blends social, moral and religious pretences.

The spectators, therefore, know exactly where they stand and can savour the spectacle when Célimène's adopts Arsinoé's pretence and turns her perfidious 'avis' against her. She returns the compliment by painting a devastating caricature of the *fausse prude*. In contrast to Arsinoé's vague insinuations, Célimène itemises facets of the prude's mask and to each affectation opposes a concrete antithesis:

> Elle est à bien prier exacte au dernier point;
> Mais elle bat ses gen, et ne les paye point.
> Dans tous les lieux dévots elle étale un grand zèle;
> Mais elle met du blanc et veut paraître belle.
> Elle fait des tableux couvrir les nudités;
> Mais elle a de l'amour pour les réalités. (939-44)

The introduction of undignified physical details is one of

Molière's favourite techniques for producing comic deflation. It provides a classic illustration of one of the general rules identified by Bergson in his theory of laughter: 'Est comique tout incident qui appelle notre attention sur le physique d'une personne alors que le moral est en cause' (7, p. 39). Célimène's riposte offers the immediate satisfaction that she adopts Arsinoé's pretence and turns it against her to unmask her hypocrisy. This is a sophisticated adaptation of the basic comedy of the biter bit. Beyond that, there is the further irony that the usually insincere Célimène is now doing precisely what Alceste advocates but is often incapable of doing himself. The counter-attack ends brilliantly in the last two couplets by returning word for word Arsinoé's hypocritical assurances of devotion.

The first round is over, and both parties recognise that Arsinoé has lost the advantage. There is a brief pause in hostilities (the ensuing four speeches: 961-74) while Arsinoé seeks to disengage from the fight. Her discomfort is evident from 'Je ne m'attendais pas à cette repartie', immediately followed in the next couplet by an unconconvincing attempt to mask her defeat:

> ... et je vois bien, par ce qu'elle a d'aigreur,
> Que mon sincère avis vous a blessé au cœur. (963-4)

Célimène, on the other hand, presses home her advantage:

> Il ne tiendra qu'à vous qu'avec le même zèle
> Nous ne continuions cet office fidèle,
> Et ne prenions grand soin de nous dire, entre nous,
> Ce que nous entendrons, vous de moi, moi de vous. (969-72)

In the second round, which begins at line 975, it is Célimène who goes on the attack. She prepares the ground with a general statement which also serves to give an unnerving warning of what is coming:

> ... chacun a raison suivant l'âge et le goût.
> Il est une saison pour la galanterie;
> Il en est une aussi propre à la pruderie. (976-8)

then plays her trump card:

> Je ne dis pas qu'un jour je ne suive vos traces:
> L'âge amènera tout, et ce n'est pas le temps,
> Madame, comme on sait, d'être prude à vingt ans. (982-4)

In a society riven by vanity and obsessed by appearances, Célimène's jibe at her adversary's age is a wounding attack. Its cruelty is only excused by the fact that Arsinoé has invited it. The latter's reply—'Certes, vous vous targuez d'un bien faible avantage' (985)—may seem feeble. All it amounts to is an unconvincing attempt to deny the importance of a fact which she can do nothing to change. But in a subtle way it also suggests that Célimène has employed a double-edged weapon. Her advantage of age is a relative one, and possibly a slight one at that. As mentioned in Chapter Two, Arsinoé's age is not made clear in the text, but the question is important for the balance of her relationship with Célimène. If Arsinoé is depicted as being well past her 'sell-by date' and wearing pathetic make-up, the role is grotesque and Célimène's taunts commensurately more cruel. If, however, we imagine her to be in her early-to-mid thirties, we are bound to reflect that Célimène's heyday is finite. When the bloom of youth fades, so will the attraction that makes her the centre of attention. Arsinoé's presence then becomes a visible reminder of how fragile Célimène's butterfly existence is, and a warning of a possible future that confronts her.

The second skirmish, then, is less conclusive than the first, though it ends (line 988) with the advantage to Célimène. Arsinoé stages a second tactical retreat:

> Et je ne sais pourquoi votre âme ainsi s'emporte,
> Madame, à me pousser de cette étrange sorte. (989-90).

Her retreat is countered by Célimène with a blocking movement:

> Et moi, je ne sais pas, Madame, aussi pourquoi
> On vous voit, en tous lieux, vous déchaîner sur moi. (991-2)

which is brilliantly converted into an attacking advance:

> Faut-il de vos chagrins, sans cesse, à moi vous prendre?
> Et puis-je mais des soins qu'on ne va pas vous rendre? (993-4)

So begins round three. As the last line quoted above implies, the real cause of Arsinoé's *dépit* is her failure with men. Having uncovered her most vulnerable weakness, Célimène turns the knife in the wound (995-8), and ends by throwing down the gauntlet:

> Vous avez le champ libre, et je n'empêche pas

Que pour les attirer, vous n'ayez des appas. (999-1000)

Once again (cf. her reaction to the taunt about her age), Arsinoé's initial response is to affect scorn and pity for Célimène (1001-1002). It is a weak and unconvincing reply, and we sense that the advantage is now very decisively in Célimène's favour. But Molière sustains dramatic tension by showing that Arsinoé is still capable of rallying for a final offensive:

> Et qu'il ne nous soit pas fort aisé de juger
> A quel prix aujourd'hui l'on peut les engager?
> Pensez-vous faire croire, à voir comme tout roule,
> Que votre seul mérite attire cette foule? (1003-1006)

In insinuating that Célimène is sexually promiscuous, she deploys a weapon capable of inflicting very real harm on Célimène's reputation in society. It is hard to know what to make of her venomous suggestions. They contribute to the carefully sustained air of mystery surrounding Célimène's behaviour. Célimène is spared the necessity to reply by Arsinoé herself: in a tactical error which throws away the advantage she has gained, she calls Célimène's bluff with a reckless piece of bravado:

> Si nos yeux enviaient les conquêtes des vôtres,
> Je pense qu'on pourrait faire comme les autres,
> Ne se point ménager, et vous faire bien voir
> Que l'on a des amants quand on veut en avoir. (1021-4)

Maladroitly, she has returned to terrain where both characters know that Célimène is unbeatable. The opportunity is too good for Célimène to miss. She repeats her earlier challenge, with a suggestion that Arsinoé is deceiving herself if she imagines herself capable of attracting males (1025-6). Abandoning the unequal struggle, the wounded rival withdraws from combat:

> Brisons, Madame, un pareil entretien:
> Il pousserait trop loin votre esprit et le mien; (1027-8)

and signals her retreat:

> Et j'aurais pris déjà le congé qu'il faut prendre,
> Si mon carrosse encor ne m'obligeait d'attendre. (1029-30).

The victor, with the unruffled and gracious manner she has preserved throughout, profits from Alceste's timely reappearance to make her excuses, thereby rescuing herself from both the *fâcheuse* and the *fâcheux*. Her parting request to Arsinoé to 'excuser [...] mon incivilité' is a triumphalist double entendre, whose real meaning is known only to the snubbed rival and the audience.

Scene 5

Alceste's arrival at this precise moment may be the product of chance (1035), but the seduction scene into which he stumbles is necessary and inevitable. It is one of the play's constant ironies that Célimène herself has inadvertently set it up for her rival. As the scene begins, we register the comic effect of Arsinoé's switch of behavioural mask from false prude to seductress. It promises the doubly savoury comedy of Arsinoé's mellifluous charm and Alceste's embarrassment at her unwelcome advances. Although Arsinoé mounts her seduction at an inauspicious moment (Alceste has just been deprived yet again of the chance to see Célimène alone) and unwittingly does everything possible to rub him up the wrong way, she nevertheless succeeds in impaling him on the hook of his own jealousy.

The basic situation is a repeat of the encounter between Alceste and Oronte in the first act. In both cases, Alceste is being courted by a self-interested flatterer. Arsinoé's opening address is a transposition into an amorous register of Oronte's. Compare the two:

> J'ai su là-bas que pour quelques emplettes
> Eliante est sortie, et Célimène aussi;
> Mais comme l'on m'a dit que vous étiez ici,
> J'ai monté pour vos dire, et d'un coeur véritable,
> Que j'ai conçu pour vous une estime incroyable... (250-4)

> Vous voyez, elle veut que je vous entretienne,
> Attendant un moment que mon carrosse vienne;
> Et jamais tous ses soins ne pouvait m'offrir rien
> Qui me fût plus charmant qu'un pareil entretien.
> En vérité, les gens d'un mérite sublime
> Entraînent de chacun et l'amour et l'estime.
> Et le vôtre sans doute a des charmes secrets
> Qui font entrer mon cœur dans tous vos intérêts. (1041-8)

For the second time we are offered the spectacle of Alceste's surprise and discomfiture at being flattered. His reaction—argumentative but comically courteous in spite of himself—is exactly what we have been led to expect.

Arsinoé compounds her first blunder by adding, as did Oronte, the prospect of advancement at Court (289-92). On this occasion, aided by Arsinoé's slowness to see how disagreeable it is, Molière allows the discussion to develop into an extended tirade against Court life (1081-98). This builds on Alceste's original criticisms of society in the first scene of the play. However, his speech is not a simple amplification of the latter. It marks a further stage in the process of withdrawal from society which will lead eventually to his *désert*. It expresses a growing awareness on his part of his incompatibility with the world:

> Et que voudriez-vous, Madame, que j'y fisse?
> L'humeur dont je me sens veut que je m'en bannisse.
> Le ciel ne m'a point fait, en me donnant le jour,
> Une âme compatible avec l'air de la cour... (1081-4)

He seems also to confuse life at Court with his own existence on the aristocratic fringes, thereby betraying an impatience to have done with both (1091-8).

Alceste's mounting anger causes comic consternation in Arsinoé. This is hardly the amorous tête-à-tête she has been trying to engineer, so she switches tack. Still wearing the mask of a solicitous friend, she steers the discussion towards Célimène's infidelity (1099 ff.) The comic climate, already tinged with a note of bitterness from Alceste's last outburst, veers towards a heightened dramatic note. Alceste is in the painful situation of confronting the most repellent embodiment of what he condemns, and finding that it is in direct conflict with his own desire for enlightenment about Célimène's conduct. His growing doubts about Célimène's fidelity and his revulsion at Arsinoé's tactics make it a moment of intense psychological drama. Molière has the task of convincing us that Alceste can overcome all his most fervently-held principles and succumb to what he plainly sees is perfidious dishonesty. We are shown his resistance crumbling in three stages. His first reaction (not without a certain *noblesse d'âme*) is to express outrage at Arsinoé's treachery:

> Mais, en disant cela, songez-vous, je vous prie,
> Que cette persone est, Madame, votre amie? (1105-1106)

Arsinoé then tempts him a second time with an even more direct accusation against Célimène:

> Oui; mais ma conscience est blessée en effet
> De souffrir plus longtemps le tort que l'on vous fait;
> L'état où je vous vois afflige trop mon âme,
> Et je vous donne avis qu'on trahit votre flamme. (1107-1110)

Alceste again rejects the temptation, but less vehemently than before. Without refuting the accusation, he retreats into sarcasm:

> C'est me montrer, Madame, un tendre mouvement,
> Et de pareils avis obligent un amant! (1111-12)

For the third time Arsinoé suggests that Célimène is deceiving Alceste (1113-15). This time his reply unconsciously betrays the fact that her insinuations have found their target:

> Cela se peut, Madame: on ne voit pas les cœurs;
> Mais votre charité se serait bien passée
> De jeter dans mon esprit une telle pensée. (1116-18)

This tacit admission provides Arsinoé with an opening which she is quick to recognise and exploit. Having offered him the bait which she knows he cannot resist, she tantalisingly pretends to withdraw it from him:

> Si vous ne voulez pas être désabusé,
> Il faut ne vous rien dire, il est assez aisé. (1119-20)

At last Alceste's urge to know the truth overcomes the repugnance he feels for Arsinoé and her manoeuvre; still contriving to concede nothing definite, he swallows the bait:

> Non; mais sur ce sujet, quoi que l'on nous expose,
> Les doutes sont fâcheux plus que tout autre chose;
> Et je ne voudrais, pour moi, qu'on ne me fît savoir
> Que ce qu'avec clarté l'on me peut faire voir. (1121-4)

Notice that Molière spares Alceste the indignity of voicing his final capitulation; instead it is expressed visually in the image of Alceste being led off-stage by Arsinoé. Confident of having hooked Alceste, Arsinoé can pretend to be acceding reluctantly to *his* wishes—'Hé bien! c'est assez dit' (1125)—before reverting to the role of seductress:

> Et si pour d'autres yeux le vôtre peut brûler,
> On pourra vous offrir de quoi vous consoler. (1131-2)

The act thus ends with the prospect of a gathering storm.

Act Four

Molière conforms to the usual practice of ending the third act on a note of suspense, to carry the drama over the interval. The fourth act, which necessarily involves a *recommencement*, rejoins the action not at the point where it left off, but with the sequel to Alceste's summons (II, 6). Philinte and Éliante are on stage. We come in on a conversation in progress.

Scene 1

The scene serves a triple purpose: to bring us up to date on the Oronte-Alceste quarrel; to redirect our attention to the central question of the Alceste-Célimène relationship, which is shortly to be brought to a climax (scene 3); and thirdly, to develop the not unrelated question of Philinte and Éliante's mutual affection. The latter serves in turn to set up the *coup de théâtre* of Alceste's offer of marriage to Éliante (scene 2). In the longer term it also prepares for her acceptance of Philinte's hand.

The affair with Oronte is dealt with in Philinte's *récit*, more than half of which takes the form of direct speech quotation where we recognise Alceste's familiar intransigence. At the end of the third act he has gone to confront the *maréchaux* vowing that 'Je ne démordrai pas, les vers sont exécrables' (765). True to his word, he is now reported as saying:

> Je le tiens galant homme en toutes les manières,
> Homme de qualité, de mérite et de cœur,
> Tout ce qu'il vous plaira, mais fort méchant auteur. (1146-8)

In short, Alceste has stood his ground, though Philinte has persuaded him to show just enough 'sentiments traitables' (766) for the affair to be ostensibly concluded (1161-2). At the same time, it leaves open the possibility of a future *rebondissement*. Oronte, denied the satisfaction of a retraction, will nurse his grudge against Alceste. Conveying that information is the first purpose of the scene.

Less obvious but equally significant is the light that is cast on Alceste himself. It is important to realise that—for the first time in the play—we are seeing Alceste through the eyes of two people who are genuinely fond of him. And the laughter, more markedly than before, is tinged with sympathy. That the *récit* is intended to evoke a comic spectacle is not in question. It brings back all the absurdity of the original storm in a teacup, accurately described by Philinte as 'bizarre' (1137). The text invites some comic impersonation of Alceste's mannerisms, though the speaker's character as an *honnête homme* precludes an exaggeratedly burlesque performance. And it is not difficult to guess that Éliante reacts to his amusement by joining in the laughter. On the other hand, it is possible to admire Alceste for standing by his opinion of the sonnet and for carrying off a victory of sorts over his presumptuous rival. The effect of all this is to cast a more favourable light on the *atrabilaire*. We are witnessing the start of a process whereby he ceases to be seen solely, or even mainly, as a comic character.

The effect is greatly intensified by Éliante's mini-portrait of Alceste. It is a distinctly attractive one, and merits some attention:

> Dans ses façons d'agir, il est fort singulier;
> Mais j'en fais, je l'avoue, un cas particulier,
> Et la sincérité dont son âme se pique
> A quelque chose, en soi, de noble et d'héroïque. (1163-6)

Notice that she distinguishes between 'ses façons d'agir' and 'son âme'. The distinction is important because it crystallises the ambivalence that characterises our reactions to Alceste from the start. But whereas the emphasis until now has been mainly on the comic aspects (the 'façons d'agir'), Éliante accentuates the positive side. She concedes that his behaviour is 'fort singulier' (echoing Philinte's epithet 'bizarre'), but she is sensitive above all to his distinctive qualities of character: sincerity, nobility, even heroism. She also confirms our earlier perception of Alceste as an *inadapté,* a man out of step with the spirit of the age:

> C'est une vertu rare au siècle d'aujourd'hui,
> Et je la voudrais voir partout comme chez lui. (1168-9)

but puts a different slant on it: the accent now is not on comic incongruity but on the exceptional nature of his qualities. In the mouth of a distinguished *femme de qualité* of the seventeenth century, this judgement must have been expected to carry considerable weight with Molière's audience.

Thinking back to Éliante's *éloge de l'amour* in Act II, praising the blindness of love to the faults of the loved one, we could be tempted to dismiss her portrait as being coloured by her love for Alceste. But her own love is hardly a blind passion; it is a rational, objective love based on esteem. In any event, the favourable picture of Alceste is delivered by a character whom we admire, and the result can only be to enhance our perception of him as a *personnage sympathique*.

A wholly comic climate is equally impossible to sustain when the conversation turns to the sentimental entanglements. Philinte raises the question of Alceste's love for Célimène, expressing surprise and misgivings just as he did when speaking to Alceste in the opening scene. Éliante's explanation that the head does not rule the heart (1175-8) echoes Alceste's own statement that 'la raison n'est pas ce qui règle l'amour' (248). As when the conversation turned to love in the first scene, Philinte's mockery gives way to friendly concern—implicit in his first speech (1169-74) and explicit later (1185-6). Célimène, too, is given a sympathetic hearing in Éliante's fair-minded reply to Philinte's musings about whether she really loves Alceste (1180-4). As she says, Célimène may not know her own feelings very well.

All this we know already, and is simply a prelude to the real issue. It is now necessary for Philinte (and the audience) to know what Éliante feels towards Alceste, and towards Philinte himself. He knows that Éliante is favourably inclined towards Alceste (215), but how much does she love him? The situation is an exquisitely delicate one for both characters. The way that they deal with it—honestly, tactfully, sensitively—offers a picture of courtly behaviour at its best. Philinte can hardly declare his own love to Éliante, knowing her inclination for Alceste. That would be to combine disloyalty to his friend with emotional blackmail. Yet honesty demands that the matter be clarified, especially now that both characters know that Alceste intends to force Célimène to declare herself that very day.

To begin with, note the extreme tact with which Philinte proceeds to sound her out. Still speaking of Alceste, he voices his fear of an emotional disaster, then continues:

> Et s'il avait mon cœur, à dire vérité,
> Il tournerait ses vœux tout d'un autre côté,
> Et par un choix plus juste, on le verrait, Madame,
> Profiter des bontés que lui montre votre âme. (1187-9)

Ostensibly the words invite Éliante to speculate on this hypothesis: *if* Alceste should come to grief with Célimène and turn to you instead (as indeed he will, imminently!), what would be *your* feelings? But the words also contain an oblique statement of his own feelings for Éliante ('s'il avait mon cœur'), thus implying an even more delicate question: and where would *I* stand?

As she says in her reply, Éliante welcomes the opportunity to voice her feelings sincerely. *Bienséance* does not allow her to respond explicitly to the last question—they are discussing her love for another man—but it is one she must have given much thought to herself. Moreover, she has registered the *sous-entendu* in Philinte's question, and both speakers are aware of its underlying significance when she gives her reply. Combining loyalty to both Célimène and Alceste, and truthfulness to her own feelings, she succeeds in conveying to Philinte what he hopes to hear (1193-6). Despite her own love for Alceste—or perhaps because of it—what she most wishes is to see his love for Célimène rewarded by marriage. Philinte, who wishes for exactly the same, is allowed to infer why. Finally, she gives Philinte to understand that if Célimène were to refuse Alceste, she could accept the prospect of being his second choice (1197-1202).

Philinte now knows where she feels her obligation to lie, and where her preference. He can therefore assure her truthfully that he does not oppose her love for Alceste: on the contrary, as a loyal friend he has even encouraged him to be more responsive to them (243-6). But, encouraged by her declaration, he can also declare his own love by saying, hypothetically, that *if* Alceste were to marry Célimène (as, it has been established, Éliante would like), *he* would be happy to be her second choice.

Scene 2

By one of those coincidences on which comedy confers an impression of inevitability, this is the moment at which Alceste bursts on to the stage. At a stroke the sentimental climate is replaced with high drama. It is a moment of crisis, identical to that in *L'Avare* where the miser discovers that he has been robbed. There is a striking similarity between Harpagon's

> Au voleur! au voleur! à l'assassin! au meurtrier! Justice, juste ciel! Je suis perdu, je suis assassiné! On m'a coupé la gorge, on m'a dérobé mon argent! (*L'Avare,* IV, 7)

and Alceste's

> ...Ah! tout est ruiné;
> Je suis, je suis trahi, je suis assassiné (1227-8)

In both situations, the central character confronts a catastrophe which strikes at the very heart of his existence. And as with *L'Avare,* the question arises: is it comic? The situation itself is not notably funny. Alceste, devastated, nearly mad with jealousy, is returning from Arsinoé's, having been shown proof of Célimène's infidelity. In other words, it is no longer a question of a bad-tempered lover picking quarrels with his mistress, but of a jealous lover who has discovered that he has been betrayed. This is not to say that he is *right*—the play goes way beyond moralising oppositions between right and wrong—but rather that his agony is *real.* This certainly makes it hard to argue for a straightforward comic interpretation. And yet... In this connection, it is worth noting that several of Alceste's speeches here (notably 1220-30) and in the following scene are taken from Molière's earlier *Dom Garcie de Navarre,* a 'serious' comedy in an elevated heroic mode. Transposed to the context of a comedy of manners, Alceste's exaggerated language (not particularly in his first outburst, but certainly in the second, third and fourth) suggests a parody of a heroic *lamento.*

In moments such as these, a comic writer's instinct is to deflect attention from feelings to gestures. It is as if the symptoms can be comic even when the disease is serious. In *L'Avare,* the miser seizes his own arm, thinking he has caught hold of the thief. In *L'École des femmes* (V, 4), Arnolphe the spurned *soupirant* utters love-lorn sighs, beats his breast and pulls at his hair. The tone of *Le Misanthrope* rules out such exaggerated effects. In a more subtle way, though, Molière does make Alceste express his suffering in symptoms which invite ridicule. He is unable to complete sentences:

> C'en est fait... Mon amour... Je ne saurais parler. (1223)
>
> Célimène... Eût-on pu croire cette nouvelle? (1229)

and twice he snaps at Philinte, telling him to mind his own business (1234, 1243-4). Neither of these undignified tics could be conceivable in genuine tragedy. And at the height of his pseudo-tragic rage, Alceste makes the most extraordinary gesture of all when he offers his love to Éliante. Or rather, flings it in her face, asking her to avenge him by marrying him.

These comic undertones are dispelled by Éliante's reply. With more gentleness than he deserves, she assures him of her affection (1260) but tries to make him see that his proposal is the product of a lover's anger (1268) and one which he will soon regret making (1262). It is as if she is offering him salvation not in the form of marriage, but by trying to introduce him into the world of *honnêteté* displayed in the preceding scene. Her real affection for him again leads us to see his suffering in a more sympathetic light. But the effect is short-lived. In a reversion to type which can only be comic, Alceste rebounds into characteristic stubborness: 'Non, non, Madame, non: l'offense est trop mortelle' (1269). Obstinacy is compounded with deafness, for he has evidently not noticed that his offer has been refused. Seeing Célimène approaching, he repeats his offering of 'un cœur tout dégagé de ses trompeurs attraits', then goes off to do battle.

Scene 3

At last Molière stages the long-awaited showdown of which we have been given a foretaste in Act II. This much admired scene is certainly one of Molière's most original. Its originality lies in the way he has adapted the comic convention of the *dépit amoureux* to the context of a psychological comedy. The *dépit amoureux,* or lovers' quarrel, is usually an independent episode which stands outside the plot, providing light relief in the form of sentimental comedy. (For example, *Tartuffe,* II, 4; *Le Bourgeois gentilhomme,* III, 10). This is not the case with the present scene, which is central to both the plot and the moral themes. It represents the culmination of Alceste's mission to re-model the world according to his own ideas. We have already seen him attempting to set society to rights, and failing comically. We are now to see his failure to mould the woman he loves to his ideal conception. For this reason, the scene also has an intense emotional charge unusual in a comedy. Indeed, some readers will question whether it is comic at all, though few would dispute that is outstanding dramatic entertainment. De Visé in 1666 was struck by the scene's unusual blend of seriousness and amusement: 'elle est toute sérieuse', he wrote, 'et cependant il y en a peu dans la pièce qui divertissement davantage' (**1**, p. 437).

In structure, the scene develops the basic model of the first quarrel, in four phases. (1) Both versions begin with an attack, which Célimène sidesteps. (2) Then the roles are reversed, with Alceste placed in the position of accused. (3) Frustrated in his objective, he can only declare his love in a climactic outburst of impotent passion. (4) On both occasions, the scene is resolved by an interruption coming from the outside world. The repetitive pattern of their behaviour is the logical and inescapable result of their incompatibility. This time, however, that incompatibility is demonstrated with such finality that although the scene ends inconclusively, we are left with the impression of having witnessed something definitive.

Looking at the scene in more detail, we can see how Molière derives a highly dramatic rhythmical structure from the psychological forces at play, and the extremely subtle blend of pathos and ridicule that it achieves.

The initial situation has the dramatic impact of an ambush which backfires. The previous scene has left Alceste emotionally primed ('Mon courroux redouble à cette approche'—1273) and promising a quarrel of epic proportions ('Je vais de sa noirceur lui faire un vif reproche, / Pleinement la confondre'—1274-5). Célimène, meanwhile, is returning to her drawing room after writing her 'mot de lettre' (1037). The encounter is bound to start on a dramatic note because of the two characters' differing expectations. Alceste's richly ironic appeal for self-control—'O Ciel! de mes transports puis-je être ici le maître?' (1277)—is an aside. The words, which convey great emotional turmoil, could be straight out of Cornelian tragedy. (They may be compared with Auguste's heroic self-mastery at the moment of ultimate provocation: *Cinna,* V, 3). But the accompanying gestures—the 'soupirs poussés' and the 'sombres regards' to which Célimène pointedly draws our attention—belong to a comic register. Alceste's first denunciation of her (taken from *Dom Garcie de Navarre*) is likewise a parody of tragedy. But Célimène's refusal to match his emotional intensity cuts the ground from under his feet. A passion so violent as Alceste's needs to be met by an equal and opposite force. Instead, Alceste finds himself pushing against a void and falls flat on his face. Célimène's ironic rejoinder, 'Voilà certainement des douceurs que j'admire', is a deflationary reminder that his extreme language and behaviour is absurdly incongruous in polite society.

So far, the encounter has followed familiar and predictable lines. Suddenly, however, Alceste's appeal for the mocking to stop introduces a serious note. We have seen him laughed at several times before, and his humourless severity has been part of the joke. His habitual response to laughter is withering scorn, which has the effect of increasing the merriment (414; 681-2). But this time, Alceste's pained 'Ah! ne plaisantez pas, il n'est pas temps de rire' produces that uncomfortable feeling when laughter dies in the throat.

The prolonged *cri de cœur* which follows is a strange mixture of passion (anger and thirst for revenge), self-justification and threats. He begins by hurling an accusation of treachery at Célimène (1287-8), withdraws partially into self-justification (1289-94), then menaces Célimène with a promise of vengeance (1295-6). Presumably the last couplet refers to his intention to marry Éliante. Naturally the threat is not made explicit, since to do so would trivialise the martyr figure he is trying to project.

Then comes the most curious part of the speech, where he attempts to rationalise his anger (1297-1308). Alceste's complaint is a typically distinctive one. It is not jealousy, though that would be an understandable reaction in the circumstances. Nor is it the pain of unrequited love: he concedes that love cannot be willed (1297-1300) and he does not hold Célimène to blame for not loving him. His objection is presented in characteristically high-minded terms: it is that Célimène has not dealt honestly with him:

> Aussi ne trouverais-je aucun sujet de plainte,
> Si pour moi votre bouche avait parlé sans feinte (1301-1302)

By relating his anger with Célimène to his ruling *passion de vérité,* Alceste may be thought to achieve a certain dignity in his suffering. It must be said, though, that it rests on a monumental misunderstanding of social conventions, as we shall see when Célimène makes her reply. It will not be long, too, before Alceste contradicts his principled stand when he appeals to Célimène to *deceive* him (1389-90).

The whole of this central part of his speech (i.e. 1297-1304) provides an emotional *diminuendo* in which Alceste is seen at his most rational. The tone is concessive and the language, for once, understated. It ends with Alceste re-stating his grievance. Notice how Molière uses that as a platform to launch the movement towards a *crescendo*. The accusation against Célimène modulates into a cry of anger:

> Mais d'un aveu trompeur voir ma flamme applaudie,
> C'est une trahison, c'est une perfidie, (1305-1306)

Anger gives rise to a repeated threat of revenge:

> Qui ne saurait trouver de grands châtiments,
> Et je puis tout permettre à mes ressentiments. (1307-1309)

This in turn unleashes an uncontrolled outburst of self-pity and menacing rage. In three symmetrical couplets, each appeal to the justice of his anger (pseudo-heroic) is precisely counterbalanced by a comically involuntary expression of its irrationality:

> Oui, oui, redoutez tout après un tel outrage;
> Je ne suis plus à moi, je suis tout à la rage:
> Percé du coup mortel dont vous m'assassinez,
> Mes sens par la raison ne sont plus gouvernés,
> Je cède aux mouvements d'une juste colère,
> Et je ne réponds plus de ce que puis faire. (1309-14)

Such a spectacular display of temper can only be followed by a descent into bathos. Célimène's cool reply (1315-16) demolishes the heroic effect of the outburst. Alceste attempts to recapture the high ground by producing the incriminating letter—a gesture of high theatricality intended to flatten Célimène conclusively. Its effect, however, is undermined when he allows himself to be drawn into quibbling over what it proves.

Célimène's mild surprise at Alceste's behaviour (1321; 1327; 1329; 1332) may be viewed as an evasive tactic. In that case, the scene becomes a straightforward stereoptyped comedy of deception. Alternatively (and far more interestingly), her surprise may be seen as real. In that case, we are witnessing a profound comedy of misunderstanding. Again, it is not a question of right and wrong, but rather a clash between two people with totally opposed views of the world. It is important to realise that *in her own eyes* Célimène is guilty of nothing. She is an unattached widow, committed to no-one. The 'crime' of which she is accused is nothing more than having encouraged her male admirers. The letter, in which Alceste sees proof of unpardonable duplicity, is therefore as innocent as it is meaningless. If anyone is 'at fault' it is Alceste, with his unwarranted bile, refusing to behave as a lover should. Hence she can honestly say, with touching indulgence: 'Vous êtes, sans mentir, un grand extravagant' (1335). Her suggestion that the letter might have been written to a female friend is entirely consistent with the logic of her position. It is surely not meant to deceive Alceste. Célimène can hardly imagine he is so unintelligent as to be taken in by anything so implausible. It must, then, be a *reductio ad absurdum* intended to expose the absurdity of his posture.

Alceste, inevitably, sees none of this, as is shown by his sarcasm (1346-50), then by his persistence in taking the suggestion literally (1351-6). It is entirely understandable that Célimène is starting to find him both insulting and tiresome.

The five speeches which follow (1356-1370) are the pivot on which the scene turns. Alceste himself triggers it when he prepares to read the letter and subject it to textual analysis. Suddenly Célimène's bemused indulgence gives way to irritation (1356-8) which, again, is not an evasive ploy, but fully justified in her eyes. We now have the inevitable comedy (inevitable because we have already seen it enacted in II, 1) of the accuser retreating in the face of Célimène's complete indifference ('Tout ce que vous croirez m'est de peu d'importance' [1362]; compare with 511-14).

Alceste's Pyrrhic victory (he has wrung from Célimène an admission that the letter was addressed to Oronte) marks the beginning of his defeat. He realises, too late, that the truth was not what he wanted to hear. Now begins the build-up to another climax in which it is hard not to detect tragic resonances. Alceste's lament:

> Ciel! rien de plus cruel peut-il être inventé?
> Et jamais cœur fut-il de la sorte traité? (1371-2)

is the same in essence as the equivalent line in the first quarrel, 'Morbleu! faut-il que je vous aime? (514), but the difference in register (especially the substitution of the more elevated 'Ciel!' for 'Morbleu!') is significant. Alceste seems to withdraw into himself. The first ten lines of his speech (1371-80) are in the form of a soliloquy which permits us to grasp the depth of his torment. Molière audaciously allows Alceste to achieve something of the painful insight of a tragic hero when he acknowledges how love is making a fool of him:

> Et cependant mon cœur est encore assez lâche
> Pour ne pouvoir briser la chaîne qui l'attache,
> Et pour ne pas s'armer d'un généreux mépris
> Contre l'ingrat objet dont il est trop épris! (1377-80)

Not that lucidity can help him to resolve his dilemma: it merely forces him to recognise the insoluble contradiction between his principles and the passion to which he is a slave. This is illustrated in the second half of his speech (1381-90) when he turns again on Célimène. Even *in extremis* Alceste still cannot quite bring himself to abandon his obsession with sincerity. The result is an absurdly contradictory plea that she cease to *appear* guilty and try instead to *appear* faithful (1386-90).

Célimène might be expected, at this point, to puncture Alceste with witty repartee (cf. 521; 525; 1285). Instead, her gentle reply produces a more subtle descent. All the same, there is a steady deflationary effect in her scolding—'Allez, vous êtes fou dans vos transports jaloux' (1391)—and in the sublime comic inversion when the coquette indignantly rejects the honest man's request that she deceive him:

> Je voudrais bien savoir qui pourrait me contraindre
> A descendre pour vous aux bassesses de feindre, (1393-4)

Having put Alceste in his place, she proceeds to turn the tables on him. Her counter-accusation (1397-1414) is built around the argument already deployed in the first quarrel, i.e. the fact of her having told Alceste she loves him should suffice to allay his unworthy suspicions. Célimène ingeniously appeals to the code of behaviour embodied in *préciosité,* with its elaborate ritual of *pudeur* on the part of the woman and respectful devotion on the part of the male (1401-1408).

The reality, as both characters must realise, is that the *précieux* code is an artificial convention with little bearing on how people actually behave. Alceste, of course, can hardly point this out without making his position much worse. Nor does he even want to disbelieve her. Hence the much-quoted and decidedly unfunny culmination of this phase of the scene, when he finally resolves to drink the poisoned cup to the end:

> Ah! traîtresse, mon faible est étrange pour vous!
> Vous me trompez sans doute avec des mots si doux;
> Mais il n'importe, il faut suivre ma destinée:
> A votre foi mon âme est tout abandonnée;
> Je veux voir, jusqu'au bout, quel sera votre cœur,
> Et si de me trahir il aura la noirceur. (1415-20)

From this elevated point, it takes only a tantalising touch of lover's pique from Célimène:

> Non, vous ne m'aimez point comme il faut que l'on aime. (1421)

to pitch Alceste into a frenzy of passion:

> Ah! rien n'est comparable à mon amour extrême... (1422)

A climax is clearly approaching, and one which is, potentially, the most moving moment in the play. In the event, loss of control makes Alceste overshoot the target. For a moment he teeters on the border between tragedy and comedy:

> Et dans l'ardeur qu'il a de se montrer à tous,
> Il va jusqu'à former des souhaits contre vous... (1423-4)

So far, so good (just). There is a short descent to comic excess:

> Oui, je voudrais qu'aucun ne vous trouvât aimable,
> Que vous fussiez réduite en un sort misérable,
> Que le Ciel, en naissant, ne vous eût donné rien,
> Que vous n'eussiez ni rang, ni naissance, ni bien... (1425-8)

Then a steady climb to the final, elated paroxysm:

> Afin que de mon cœur l'éclatant sacrifice
> Vous pût d'un pareil sort réparer l'injustice,
> Et que j'eusse la joie et la gloire, en ce jour,
> De vous voir tenir tout des mains de mon amour. (1429-32)

What distinguishes comedy from tragedy is not subject matter but context and perspective. Given a different time and place, Alceste's outburst could be tragically felt. In a seventeenth-century drawing room, spoken to a coquette, it is highly incongruous. For readers, the text may have a disembodied quality that enables them to respond mainly to the emotional charge of the words, though spectators have before them a visual reminder of the context. As readers, we can also reflect that Alceste's behaviour is objectively implausible. Molière's remarkable achievement is firstly to have convinced spectators of its psychological truth, and secondly to make them disregard the context sufficiently to respond to it at an emotional level. Until, that is, Célimène's brilliant reply restores a normal perspective:

> C'est me vouloir du bien d'une étrange manière!
> Me préserve le ciel que vous ayez matière... (1433-4)

The return to irony signals a disengagement from the emotional *face à face* and brings the scene back to its starting point. It underlines something which is obvious to us, if not to the characters: that for all the words which have been expended, they are trapped in a relationship which cannot evolve from within. (It will be the business of the dénouement to bring new information to light to break the impasse.) For that reason, their dispute is not resolved but brought to a halt by the arrival of du Bois.

Scene 4

Structurally, this short scene completes the pattern laid down in the first three acts, each of which ends with Alceste frustrated in his efforts to speak with Célimène (by Oronte in Act I, the *maréchaux* in Act II, and Arsinoé in Act III). Ostensibly its function is to tell us that there has been a development in Alceste's lawsuit (1453) and that the outcome is unfavourable. As far as the action is concerned, the scene is superfluous, since V, 1 tells us all we need to know on that score. Its true dramatic value, of course, lies in providing light comic relief after the serious and emotionally intense scene with Célimène. It introduces the only element of farce in a comedy which is otherwise notable for its uniformly elevated tone.

As one might expect from a playwright steeped in the tradition of farce, the scene is by means negligible. It is announced by an incongruous apparition of a flustered servant 'plaisamment figuré'. This is usually interpreted as boots, coachman's hat, gauntlets, whip, coach-horn, etc. The suggestion is that du Bois is melodramatically equipped as a postillion ready to help Alceste flee from arrest. The idea of the incompetent messenger may have been borrowed from Quinault's *L'Amant indiscret* (1654) where a servant searches for a letter he was bringing, and finally declares it to be lost. Molière exploits the idea to its maximum with a succession of varied comic efects: the servant's initial obscurity, hesitations and digressions, building to a false revelation (the letter), suspense while he searches for the letter (a classic *lazzo*), and final collapse when it transpires he has forgotten to bring it. De Visé rightly said of this modest little scene that 'l'esprit paraît aussi bien dans les petites choses que dans les grandes' (**1**, p. 438). There is superior wit in the way Molière has integrated a farcical interlude into the comedy of character. The full flavour of the situation derives less from Alceste's desire to know the contents of the message than from its untimely occurrence and the recipient's character. A servant's procrastination is infinitely more funny when the victim is an *atrabilaire,* and when we know what is really on his mind.

Alceste's parting words to Célimène:

souffrez à mon amour
De vous revoir, Madame, avant la fin du jour. (1479-80)

project the action towards its impending climax.

Act Five

Analysis of the act

The purpose of the final act is to draw all the threads together into a *nœud,* then to untie the knot. In *Le Misanthrope*— unusually for Molière—the dénouement is achieved without recourse to artificial procedures of a *deus ex machina* type (i.e. without an external agent). All the material necessary for the action to be resolved is present in the intrigue and the psychology as it has been laid out. This confers on the final events an impression of inevitability—but not without dramatic suspense, which Molière prolongs to the very last moment, nor without a number of surprises.

The act begins with a steady tightening of the knot (scenes 1-3). There is a sensation that events are gathering pace. In the interval between the acts a number of developments have occurred. Alceste has received confirmation that his lawsuit has gone against him. Moreover, his opponent has circulated rumours that Alceste is the author of a 'livre abominable'. Oronte, too, has been pursuing his vendetta by lending his weight to the rumour. As a result of these combined blows, Alceste's hatred of mankind is aggravated to such a pitch that he has now resolved to quit society and intends to ask Célimène to join him. Thus the two secondary intrigues (the lawsuit and the long-running quarrel with Oronte) are made to converge and are brought to bear to force a resolution to the central issue (i.e. the now inseparable matters of Alceste's misanthropy, and his relationship with Célimène). Oronte arrives (scene 2), asking Célimène to reject Alceste in his favour. Alceste confronts them both and demands that Célimène choose between them. The arrival of Eliante and Philinte (scene 3), then of Acaste, Clitandre and Arsinoé (scene 4) completes the gathering for a theatrical finale.

The unravelling process (scene 4) comes in two phases, and takes the form of a succession of *coups de théâtre*. In the first phase the secondary issues are disposed of. Célimène's indiscreet letters are produced, supplying the first *coup de théâtre*. Acaste, Clitandre, Oronte extract their revenge, Célimène is publicly humiliated for her deception, and

Arsinoé, too, is rebuffed by Alceste. The secondary characters withdraw, leaving the protagonists to resolve the central issue. Still Molière prolongs the uncertainty. Instead of the exploding in rage, Alceste forgives Célimène, (second *coup de théâtre*). His love is too strong for him to abandon her, and he asks her to marry him—a surprising outcome in relation to his misanthropy, but a logical one in relation to what we have seen in the last love scene. Conversely, he attaches to the proposal an intolerable condition: that she withdraw from society and join him in his *désert*—an unrealistic expectation, yet one which is, again, psychologically consistent in relation to his misanthropy. Célimène's rejection of the proposal, which is equally inevitable, is accompanied by an offer of marriage without strings attached. Célimène having offered to meet him half-way, Alceste now must choose to accept this or nothing. This decision constitutes the dénouement proper, which has been delayed until the last possible moment—the final twenty-nine lines of the play—and still reserves some suprises. Suddenly (third *coup de théâtre*) Alceste's love is extinguished. He revokes his offer to Célimène, who now withdraws. Turning to Eliante he asks to be released from his earlier offer of marriage (fourth *coup de théâtre*) and opts finally for solitude. Philinte and Eliante are now free to announce their marriage—the traditional ending to a comedy—while Alceste leaves for his *désert,* pursued by his loyal friends.

Molière has often been criticised for the weakness of his dénouements, which are said to be artificial and unconvincing. Although *Le Misanthrope* generally escapes the charge of being contrived, its failure to provide a final solution is sometimes felt to be unsatisfactory. But the last act of *Le Misanthrope* is an artistic triumph on every level. In terms of dramatic impact, as the foregoing outline suggests, it is a technical *tour de force.* As for the uncertainty surrounding the final image, about which more will be said later, surely it is the only realistic outcome to an insoluble human dilemma. Spectators who recognise that real life is too complex to admit of simple solutions, and who appreciate the potentiality of art to suggest rather than to reduce life to simple dimensions, will not try to explain it away.

Scene 1

As is usual in a classical play, the first scene of the final act suspends the action while the protagonist takes stock of his position. In terms of dramatic rhythm it is felt as a lull before the storm bursts. We find we are back to the situation presented at the beginning of the play: Alceste is fulminating against the world and Philinte is attempting to reason with him. The pattern of their dialogue naturally repeats that of the first scene, namely: Alceste holds forth in tirades, which are punctuated by shorter interjections from Philinte. On four occasions Philinte is interrupted in mid-sentence. In other words, we have the characteristic rhythm of an *atrabilaire* speaking to a reasonable man. The same rhythm also gives the scene its physical movement. It is easy to imagine how Alceste's irritation is automatically expressed in restless motion; de Visé, who can only have been describing a recollection of Molière's performance as Alceste, wrote of 'son chagrin, qui l'oblige à se promener et rêver' (**1**, p. 439).

By replaying the original debate at this point, Molière allows us to see how Alceste's original ideas are faring now that they have been tested against reality. In every respect his views of man and society are unchanged. All is 'perversité', 'fausseté noire', 'trahison', 'imposture', echoing his statement in the first scene that:

> Je ne trouve partout que lâche flatterie,
> Qu'injustice, intérêt, trahison, fourberie. (93-4)

What has evolved is not his perception of the world but his response to it. Our first sight of Alceste was of a man in combative spirit. In setting forth his ideas to Philinte he was declaring war on society. Now he recognises the futility of his mission. This makes Alceste unusual, among Molière's monomaniacs, in having learned something from his experiences. The lesson he has learnt, though, is a narrow one. It excludes the most obvious lesson of all, which is that he may have been wrong. All he has learnt is that he is not made for life in society:

> La raison, pour mon bien, veut que je me retire:
> Je n'ai point sur ma langue un assez grand empire.
> De ce que je dirais je ne répondrais pas,
> Et je me jetterais cent choses sur les bras (1573-6)

As a result, the idea of retreating from the world, which in the first scene took the form of a vague intimation (143-4), is now presented as an irrevocable decision.

With the repeated clash of ideas is revived all the original ambiguity of Alceste's cult of virtue. On the one hand we have to recognise that he has indeed been wronged by his adversaries. Yet the more he parades his legitimate grievances, the more he distances himself from the spectator. Once again, we see the childish satisfaction he derives from having proof of man's dishonesty:

> Ce sont vingt mille francs qu'il m'en pourra coûter,
> Mais pour vingt mille francs j'aurai droit de pester
> Contre l'iniquité de la nature humaine,
> Et de nourrir pour elle une immortelle haine. (1547-50)

And once again we witness his total failure to see matters in their proper perspective. The self-knowledge that leads him to see the consequences of his behaviour is coupled with moumental blindness. As Philinte points out, the harm done to Alceste is objectively not great. No-one takes seriously the rumours spread by his adversaries (1526-8; 1535-7), and as for the lawsuit, an appeal may redress matters (1539-40). It might be objected that Philinte's pragmatism is missing the moral point (the point being that the rumours are malicious and that justice has manifestly failed to be done). Perhaps that is why Molière allows him to justify his phlegmatism in terms of a higher moral philosophy (1561-9).

Above all, we see once again how Alceste's idealism is rooted in egocentricity. It is surely absurd, as Alceste imagines, that this commonplace occurence constitutes an outrage of such magnitude that it will be seen by posterity as proof of man's iniquity. Nor is it reasonable to equate the little clique of adversaries with the entire human race (1517). Alceste's error, finally, is to confuse his own microsociety with the whole of mankind

If, therefore, we ask where Molière's sympathies lie, or where he expected the audience's sympathies to lie, the answer has to be the same as in the first scene. Molière is again presenting us with the paradox of a man committed to virtue but rendered ridiculous by egocentricity, inflexibility and excess. Our abiding impression is of a man who is wilfully deaf to reason:

> Non, vous avez beau faire et beau me raisonner,
> Rien de ce que je dis ne me peut détourner: (1483-4)

> Je sais que vous parlez, Monsieur, le mieux du monde;
> En beaux raisonnements vous adonnez toujours;
> Mais vous perdez le temps et tous vos beaux discours. (1570-2)

So the scene ends with the wounded Alceste withdrawing into his 'petit coin sombre'. It is an extraordinarily poignant image of self-inflicted isolation, and would be tragic if we shared Alceste's view of himself. Only Philinte's presence ensures the kind of perspective which allows us to recognise its absurdity.

Scenes 2 & 3

With the arrival of Célimène and Oronte, the action resumes, and begins an accelerating movement towards the climax. Although we have known since the fourth act that Oronte is one of Célimène's suitors, his eagerness to marry her (1587-8) may come as a surprise. The motive quickly becomes clear: it is pure spite. He urges her:

> ...de ne plus souffrir qu'Alceste vous prétende,
> De le sacrifier, Madame, à mon amour,
> Et de chez vous enfin le bannir dès ce jour (1594-6)

Oronte's laughable transparency prevents the scene from sliding into *drame*. The scene involves a subtle comedy of unmasking made more piquant by the fact that it is accidentally witnessed by his rival. No less ironic is the fact that Alceste is seeing a miniature re-enactment of his own quarrel with Célimène when he asked her to give up his rivals.

Alceste's emergence from his corner is a masterly theatrical moment. It combines Bergsonian comedy of automatism (the jack-in-the-box effect of someone unable to contain himself) with a powerful *coup de théâtre*. At a stroke, a situation from which a skilful coquette can easily extricate herself is transformed into a tense and dangerous one. Célimène's game depends on playing each of her various suitors off separately against the rest. But a classic feature of comedy is that characters who should at all costs be kept apart run into each other—and this is precisely what happens here. The sense of a net closing on Célimène is conveyed theatrically by a rapid sequence of symmetrical *répliques* (1609-22). Her first couplet (1623-4), rising above the clamour, instils silence and directs the spectators' attention to her next words. In a similar situation in *Dom Juan* (II, 5) the profligate lover confronts two women to whom he has promised marriage and farcically succeeds in convincing each of them that she is the favoured one. Célimène attempts the same ploy (1625-8), and, interestingly, tries to sustain it by saying it would be unseemly and hurtful to reject the unsuccessful lover in the presence of the other (1629-36). This is an ingenious abuse of *honnêteté* in defence of insincerity. Philinte, speaking as a perfect *honnête homme,* has argued that there are times when it is preferable to suppress the truth rather than give offence needlessly (73-80). Alceste's refusal to heed this sensible advice has given rise to much laughter at his expense. But for a coquette to take refuge behind *honnêteté* when faced with two lovers who are determined to settle for nothing less than absolute sincerity, is derisively irrelevant.

Neither lover is deceived by the evasion, though typically, it is Alceste who says so: 'Conserver tout le monde est votre grande étude' (1641). As a result, the clamour resumes and continues to a second crescendo (line 1648). Éliante's arrival (scene 3) brings a brief respite. Célimène looks to her for reinforcement, still trying her sustain the pretence that only a delicate concern for *bienséance* prevents her from speaking the truth (1659). Éliante's reply introduces the perspective of the genuine *honnête femme* (1660-2). As we have seen (1180-4) she is not unsympathetic to Célimène, but when asked to support her insincerity she declines. In three lines of unaffected directness she demolishes Célimène's pseudo-*honnête* scruples, and so encourages Alceste and Oronte to resume the attack. Six staccato lines push the scene to its third and final crescendo.

Scene 4

Acaste and Clitandre appear, but the action runs on without a break. Four lines suffice to establish the new alignment of characters. In an interesting inversion of the grouping in the first salon scene, Célimène is again the focus of the other characters' attention. But it is hostility, not admiration that draws them to her. Acaste puts Célimène in the dock (1669-70), and Clitandre's couplet making common cause with Oronte and Alceste draws them into the line-up for the prosecution (1671-2). Thus Molière ensures that the arrival of Acaste and Clitandre builds on the tension of the previous scene rather than dissipates it. Having done that, he can allow himself the leisure of satire at the expense of Arsinoé, who completes the line-up. She offers once again the spectacle of her own version of insincerity. In their various ways, each of the characters illustrates how language is used by intelligent people as a mask. Arsinoé's speciality, as we have already seen, is a systematic and blatant inversion of the truth. Our enjoyment as spectators comes from seeing through the mask, which we do by deciphering the unspoken subtext in what the characters say. In Arsinoé's case this is a straightforward matter of reading black for white.

Célimène's unmasking arises as a consequence of the pact agreed by the two *marquis* in III, 1. That, of course, is merely the dramatic contrivance Molière employs to bring about the punishment which satire demands. The real author of her disgrace is Célimène herself who is now reaping the rewards of a social career built on *médisance*. Her indiscretion in committing her *médisances* to paper suggests a confident risk-taker who finally overreaches herself. Her undoing is all the more effective for its rapidity and the clinical efficiency with which her victims extract their revenge. The veneer of politeness gives it added spice. The reading of her letters is both structurally and thematically a counterpart to the *scène des portraits,* but this time Célimène's genius for portraiture is turned against her and no-one on stage is laughing. As for the spectators, they are invited to laugh at all and sundry, with the possible exception of Alceste. The two marquises are so consumed in pique that they fail to see that they are acting against themselves by reading out Célimène's very accurate portraits of them. Within the letters themselves, everyone receives his 'paquet' and is thus exposed to ridicule. Molière even gives himself the luxury of a memorable supernumerary portrait, that of the bizarre 'flandrin de vicomte' passing the hours by spitting into a well. Célimène's defeat is poetic justice in the form of a classic comic situation: that of 'the biter bit'. Arsinoé's turn will come shortly. For the moment she is present as a gloating spectator.

As the three offended lovers withdraw they enact the inevitable ritual of abuse (1691-1706). In doing so, they retain their basic character types to the very last. Our final sight of them is of three carefully nuanced variations on the theme of vanity: disdain (Clitandre), scorn (Acaste), indignation (Oronte). Their punishment (which after all is not very grave) is perfectly fitted to their crime: for the social vice of vanity they are wounded in their pride. Oronte's parting shot addressed to Alceste wraps up their quarrel:

> Monsieur, je ne fais plus d'obstacle à votre flamme,
> Et vous pouvez conclure l'affaire avec Madame. (1707-1708)

It also neatly supplies the cue for Arsinoé to step in to pick up the spoils. Molière now dispenses justice to Arsinoé (and in the process inflicts a final indignity on Alceste) and he makes it humorous. Her exaggerated shock at Célimène's behaviour (1709-11) is irresistibly comic, as is the patent ulterior motive in her pointed flattery of Alceste:

> Je ne prends point de part aux intérêts des autres;
> Mais Monsieur, que chez vous fixait votre bonheur,
> Un homme comme lui, de mérite et d'honneur,
> Et qui vous chérissait avec idolâtrie,
> Devait-il... (1712-16).

(To suggest that Alceste idolises Célimène is really larding the cake!). Alceste tells her to mind her own business, then brutally rips off her mask to expose her real motive:

> Et ce n'est pas à vous que je pourrai songer
> Si par un autre choix je cherche à me venger. (1721-2)

and to produce a laughable volte-face from Arsinoé:

> Hé! croyez-vous, Monsieur, qu'on ait cette pensée
> Et que de vous avoir on soit tant empressée? (1723-4)

The amusement fades somewhat as she turns her venom on Célimène (1727-8). Her exit lines:

> Vous ferez bien encore de soupirer pour elle,
> Et je brûle de voir une union si belle. (1731-2)

show her spiteful to the end. As well as rounding off the portrayal of her character, they supply a clever liaison by turning the spotlight on to the main characters.

As Arsinoé withdraws, the satirical mood fades away and a highly charged climate sets in. Neither Alceste nor Célimène has spoken a word throughout the preceding events. We know that they must now face each other, and we sense that it will be painful. What follows is predictable in a way, yet full of surprises. We will witness first, a process of convergence when for a few moments the two characters sustain an illusion that they can resolve their difference; and then the inevitable separation that follows from their realisation of their final, irremediable incompatibility.

A cry of rage from Alceste is entirely possible, and seems about to happen. But histrionic choler would turn the moment of truth into another undignified scene. Instead, Molière gives us something more subtle. Alceste gives a signal that the long-suppressed rage is about to burst out:

> Ai-je pris sur moi-même un assez long empire,
> Et puis-je maintenant?... (1735-6)

but he is disarmed by Célimène's quiet confession:

> Oui, vous pouvez tout dire;
> Vous en êtes en droit, lorsque vous vous plaindrez,
> Et de me reprocher tout ce que vous voudrez.
> J'ai tort, je le confesse, et mon âme confuse
> Ne cherche à vous payer d'aucune vaine excuse. (1736-40)

It is a masterly stroke that the mechanism here is identical to that which was used in the two quarrel scenes. As on those occasions, Célimène admits she has wronged Alceste—but this time she is sincere. Or so it would seem. In fact, for all the apparent sincerity of her words, there remains something impenetrable for the spectator. Is this a genuine 'moment of truth', or another evasion? Possibly neither. Célimène assures Alceste that her feelings for him are different, that the other men mean nothing to her (1741-2). We cannot avoid reflecting that she implies as much to every man with whom she flirts. Still, we can, if we choose, believe that for once she is speaking sincerely: there is certainly nothing to disprove it. But neither do we have any conclusive evidence to dispel our doubts. Our surest touchstone is Éliante's wise observation that:

> Son cœur de ce qu'il sent n'est pas bien sûr lui-même;
> Il aime quelquefois sans qu'il le sache bien,
> Et croit aimer aussi parfois qu'il n'en est rien. (1182-4)

The one mistake, therefore, would be to try to dispel the enigma, for it would be impossible to do so without destroying the character's *vraisemblance*. It seems to me intolerable that Célimène, with her seductive charm, grace and lightness of touch, could descend to a vulgar deceit. But neither is it plausible to imagine a profound transformation in a character whose very essence is her shallowness. Fallen women redeemed by love, and reformed characters generally, belong not to comedy but to melodramas and morality tales.

The 'truth' here is presumably Célimène's truth, delivered with all the sincerity of which she is capable, and all the limitations of a selfish and superficial person. She is apparenty fond of Alceste ('il me divertit quelquefois'), and perhaps more so than of her other suitors, genuinely if momentarily, now that she sees the hurt she has caused him. It is possible to read into her words a flash of insight into his pain. On the other hand, the feelings she explicitly attributes to him are not suffering but 'courroux' and 'ressentiment' (1741; 1743), suggesting that all she really sees is another effect of 'ses brusqueries et son chagrin bourru'.

If her feelings for Alceste remain elusive, the sincerity of her confession is also inscrutable. Although she appears unequivocally repentant—'J'ai tort, je le confesse [...] je tombe d'accord de mon crime envers vous' (1739; 1742)—she also seems to be casting doubt on the extent of her guilt, as the supplied italics indicate:

> Votre ressentiment, *sans doute,* est raisonnable;
> Je sais combien *je dois vous paraître* coupable.
> Que toute chose dit que *j'ai pu* vous trahir... (1743-5)

Is this a deliberate evasion? Is she excusing herself? Or even trying to make Alceste doubt her guilt? A more interesting interpretation is that while recognising that Alceste finds her behaviour reprehensible, she has no real sense herself that what she has done is wrong. It is entirely fitting, and a tribute to Molière's psychological perception, that at this moment of truth Célimène escapes us, and possibly escapes herself. She is simply remaining true to an essence which is built entirely on appearances.

Her confession produces the illusion that the gap between the two characters is narrowing. Alceste will now attempt to bridge the gap. Her invitation (or challenge?) to Alceste to hate her (1746-7) turns the spotlight on to him. Célimène's social ostracism, which Alceste so desired ('je voudrais qu'aucun ne vous trouvât aimable', etc.—1425 ff.), has now come about. It remains to be seen what advantage he can take of it. From the start of the play we have seen him struggling with an impossible contradiction between a passion for truth and a passion for Célimène. Reason demands that he must finally choose between them. But psychological necessity dictates that he is unable to sacrifice either one or the other. Instead, he attempts to square the circle. The bargain he proposes combines lucidity and irrationality to the highest degree. Alceste himself expresses awareness of its irrationality in the 'aside' to Éliante and Philinte which seems to prepare for a capitulation (1751-6). Then comes what he would like to believe is a transcendent leap, shot through with unconscious Christian symbolism. He offers her forgiveness, believing that his sacrifice will open the path to her repentance and redemption:

> C'est par là seulement que, dans tous les esprits,
> Vous pouvez réparer le mal de vos écrits,
> Et qu'après cet éclat, qu'un noble cœur abhorre,
> Il peut m'être permis de vous aimer encore. (1765-8)

Needless to say, this impossible future presupposes a very different Célimène from the shallow and selfish woman she really is. The offer is only made possible by Alceste's blindness to her real nature. It also conceals a monumental self-deception. His 'capitulation' is nothing of the sort: it depends on Célimène accepting the offer on his terms. His 'sacrifice' is an attempt to satisfy a selfish concept of love which demands total and exclusive possession. In effect, he is asking Célimène to sacrifice herself to his love and his principles.

Célimène's horrified reaction:

> Moi, renoncer au monde avant que de vieillir,
> Et dans votre désert aller m'ensevelir! (1769-70)

is all that is needed to bring home the utter futility of Alceste's proposal. So begins the inevitable polarisation of the two characters. Alceste's reluctance to admit defeat:

> Eh! s'il faut qu'à mes feux votre flamme réponde,
> Que vous doit importer tout le reste du monde?
> Vos désirs avec moi ne sont-ils pas contents? (1771-3)

is wholly understandable. Its effect, however, is to underline the egoism of his love and the extent of the sacrifice he is asking of Célimène. It also obliges Célimène to justify her refusal, and leads her to make her own counter-offer of marriage without strings:

> La solitude effraye une âme de vingt ans:
> Je ne sens point la mienne assez grande, assez forte,
> Pour me résoudre à prendre un dessein de la sorte.
> Si le don de ma main peut contenter vos voeux,
> Je pourrai me résoudre à serrer de tels nœuds;
> Et l'hymen... (1774-9)

These are the last words Célimène speaks, and the

impression they leave is a distinctly favourable one. Her reasons for being unable to withdraw from the world are understandable. She is the consummate social creature for whom renunciation of the world amounts to nothing less than a form of suicide. The offer of her hand is hardly passionate, but its generosity should not be underestimated. For a young, attractive pleasure-seeking widow to relinquish her enviable independence to any husband, let alone one as irascible and censorious as Alceste, represents a greater sacrifice than any which Alceste has been capable of. Paradoxically, the *générosité* of her last words brings her closer here to embodying the social ideal of *honnêteté* than could ever have been imagined.

A further effect of this is to throw into greater relief the ungracious way in which Alceste finally rejects her. There is more than a suggestion here of the mechanical reversion to type so typical of Molière's obsessionals:

> Non: mon cœur à présent vous déteste,
> Et ce refus lui seul fait plus que tout le reste.
> Puisque vous n'êtes point, en des liens si doux,
> Pour trouver tout en moi, comme moi tout en vous,
> Allez, je vous refuse, et ce sensible outrage
> De vos indignes fers pour jamais me dégage. (1779-84)

Ultimately the obsession controls the man. Alceste's imaginary ideal world allows no room for a person such as Célimène, and he ends, as he must, by rejecting her: not for anything she has *done,* but for being what she *is.* But has she ever pretended to be anything else?

Célimène's exit marks the resolution of the first issue (Alceste's relationship with her), and points to the resolution of the second (his relationship with society). First the remaining emotional threads must be disentangled. Although the general climate is serious and subdued, we are allowed the humorous spectacle of Alceste's embarrassment as he deals with his impetuous fourth-act promise of marriage to Éliante. The movement is clearly towards separation, but Molière allows some dramatic uncertainty to creep in. At first Alceste appears to be repeating the proposal (1785-7), then he retracts it (1788-95) with considerably more humility than he showed to Célimène. Éliante allows him to wallow in his awkward apology for a while (1791-5) before cutting in sharply to detach herself from him and accept Philinte's proposal instead. This strand of the intrigue is thus resolved, as it should be, with the conventional prospect of marriage. Alceste gives the union his blessing (though it hardly requires it!):

> Puissiez-vous, pour goûter de vrais contentements,
> L'un pour l'autre à jamais garder ces sentiments! (1801-1802)

This could be read as generous well-wishing, but it is hardly likely. I think it is surely intended to be much more than the usual polite platitude. If we read it as an unspoken expression of misanthropic pessimism and self-pity, it supplies the necessary springboard into the superb exit lines:

> Trahi de toutes parts, accablé d'injustices,
> Je vais sortir d'un gouffre où triomphent les vices,
> Et chercher sur la terre un endroit écarté
> Où d'être homme d'honneur on ait la liberté. (1803-1806)

Alceste's departure is the saddest exit of any of Molière's characters. It has the poignancy of Charlie Chaplin's early films where the solitary funny man walks off into the distance, consoling himself with a derisive gesture to the world. But whatever emotions his words evoke—and some readers will find them very moving indeed—it would be a mistake to think of them as tragic. Instead we should admire the perfect harmony with which Molière resolves the varied emotions that Alceste has aroused throughout the play. Admiration, sympathy and wry amusement are held in exact counterpoise. Alceste's disaffection with society culminates in a Jansenist pessimism which leads him to reject the world as a 'gouffre où triomphent les vices'. But that view, tragic though it is, is inseparable from the man's character, which remains consistent to the end. As well as containing much that is laudable, it also includes the stubbornness, blindness and self-inflicted isolation of the archetypal comic character. It has been argued that Alceste's realisation of his failure singles him out from other Moliéresque characters and makes him an increasingly tragic figure at the end of the play. Personally I can detect no awareness on Alceste's part of his own error, only an aggravated conviction of his own rightness. It is the classic comic syndrome of the man who, as Howarth says, 'retreats into a fantasy world of his own in which he is right and the rest of humanity are wrong' (**28**, p. 103). The four lines quoted above contains all the hallmarks of egocentricity: lack of perspective, self-dramatisation, a certain elated satisfaction in his own martyrdom, the projection of himself as a superior being. We should also be conscious that his exile is as much the result of his own irrationality as of the world's imperfections. In the world as it is, Alceste's cult of virtue is an unreasonable one: in the words of the eminently sensible Philinte, a *folie:*

> ...c'est une folie à nulle autre seconde
> De vouloir se mêler de corriger le monde. (157-8)

The last words of the play also go to Philinte:

> Allons, Madame, allons employer toute chose,
> Pour rompre le dessein que son cœur se propose. (1807-1808)

This final couplet is sometimes omitted or thrown away in performance. Arnavon calls it a 'distique banal et plat' and suppresses it because it is incompatible with his vision of 'l'Alceste-géant, type, à la fois, d'homme et de surhomme' (**12**, p. 273). Critics and producers who share this view of Alceste naturally prefer to see the misunderstood and much-abused hero departing in silence. Yet this is clearly not at all what Molière intended. Philinte's words are there to redress the balance, and to remind us that Alceste's exile is no more reasonable than the reforming crusade he has now abandoned. One of the many paradoxes in the central character is that for all his professed hatred of society, he needs society to justify his misanthropy. Everything that motivates him—his superiority complex, his *soif de distinction,* his urge to judge and criticise other people, his argumentativeness—feeds on human contact. It is not hard to see that the *désert* will be as intolerable to Alceste as the society he shuns. His final vision of 'un endroit écarté / Où d'être homme d'honneur on ait la liberté' expresses the contradiction of an unsociable man trying to live out a social ideal without society.

Our last sight, then, is of Alceste fleeing from society—but with Philinte (now accompanied by Éliante) again exercising a moderating influence. The situation echoes the ending of the first act, and provides an inverted mirror image of the play's opening movement. Philinte's last words are thus a crucial element in the overall pattern. They bring the action back to its starting point:

PHILINTE —Qu'est-ce donc? Qu'avez-vous?

ALCESTE —Laissez-moi, je vous prie.

and keep alive the cycle of indecision and false exits that has marked Alceste's behaviour throughout. In this way Molière brings the play to a close with an unusual dramatic pattern combining a traditional fifth-act dénouement with a cyclical movement which suggests it could all start up again. This seems to me an eminently satisfying outcome both dramatically and from the point of truth. Indeed, it is the only realistic outcome to the drama of the supremely paradoxical creature which Molière has invented: a fish which cannot abide water, nor live out of water.

Conclusion

I began by mentioning some of the controversial issues of interpretation raised by *Le Misanthrope:* is Alceste intended as an object of ridicule? and what is the lesson of the play? The answer to the first of these questions is implicit in my Commentary: it is unequivocally 'yes'. In fact, of course, there is no such thing as an objective or neutral interpretation of this or any other play. Each reader, or director, will put his or her own slant on the characters and find different patterns of meaning in the play. Humour, too, is a subjective matter. As we have seen, Alceste's ridicule does not exclude a measure of sympathy, and it is for each reader to decide where the exact balance lies. Nevertheless, when the character is viewed in his social context, and when attention is paid not only to what he says but also to the manner in which he says it, Molière's comic intentions could hardly be more clear. One of the most inescapable motifs throughout the play is the way in which Alceste's 'bizarrerie' makes him a recurrent source of amusement to his peers. Some may find this intolerable and seek to elevate Alceste to a heroic status. But that is to overturn a basic premiss of the play, which is that in polite society of the seventeenth century Alceste's humourless pontificating is, and can only be, comically incongruous.

This is not to equate laughter with triviality, nor to suggest that the comedy functions only at the level of entertainment. All comedy is serious, in that it deals with the imperfections of the world. Satire obviously implies criticism, and laughter in general is often thought to be a form of punishment. According to Bergson, laughter operates as a 'social gesture' whose purpose is to reprimand unsociable behaviour (**7**, p. 15). In the French theatre of the seventeenth century a similar idea was expressed in the formula *castigat ridendo mores*—punishment by laughter. Molière himself appeared to subscribe to this idea during the 'Querelle de *Tartuffe*', when he wrote that 'le devoir de la comédie [est] de corriger les hommes en les divertissant' (*Tartuffe,* Premier Placet). But it is questionable whether this should be taken as anything more than an appeal to a conventional platitude. In fact, no-one has ever succeeded in demonstrating that laughter is effective in causing people to modify their behaviour. Watching a play by

Molière, we can readily identify the foibles of our friends and acquaintances but are less disposed, I think, to see ourselves as the object of ridicule. Apart from the polemical statements made in defence of *Tartuffe,* there is little evidence that Molière believed that laughter could change people's behaviour. All the evidence of his plays suggests a more sceptical resignation to the human condition. He implicitly recognises this in *Le Misanthrope* by presenting Alceste's condition as incurable.

As for the play's lesson, then, this has to be understood not in the narrow sense of prescriptions for good behaviour, but in terms of promoting a more accurate perception of the world. No doubt this includes a recognition of the imperfections of human nature. This pleasurable recognition, stemming from a comic perspective on the world, forms the first lesson. But it also includes an awareness of the folly of trying to reform the world. The play amply confirms Philinte's warning that 'Le monde par vos soins ne se changera pas' (103). La Rochefoucauld identified the vanity of what we might call the Alceste syndrome: 'L'orgueil a plus de part que la bonté aux remontrances que nous faisons à ceux qui commettent des fautes, et nous ne les reprenons pas tant pour les en corriger, que pour leur persuader que nous en sommes exempts' (Maxime 37). So the second lesson, if we are to escape Alceste's comic fate, is that 'A force de sagesse, on peut être blâmable' (150). True wisdom, it suggests, lies not in perceiving the faults of the world but in learning to live with them. Molière's wisdom, and the final lesson of the play, is to remind us that in 'ce grand Hôpital des Incurables', as La Mothe le Vayer called the world, 'il n'y en a point de plus fous que ceux qui veulent faire les Médecins.' This may seem a strange conclusion for a satirist. But it is the reflection of a clear-sighted observer of human nature who recognises the limitations of satire, while inviting us to enjoy his demonstration of the simple but profound truth that 'Les hommes, la plupart, sont étrangement faits!' (*Tartuffe,* l. 339).

Bibliography

Place of publication of books is Paris, unless otherwise indicated.

Editions

1. Molière — *Œuvres Complètes*, ed. E. Despois & F. Mesnard. Hachette, 1873-1900, 13 vols (vol. 5).

2. *Le Misanthrope* — ed. G. Rudler. Oxford: Blackwell, 1962.

3. ——— — eds. Charles Bouton & René Jasinski. Marcel Didier, 1962.

4. ——— — ed. E. Lop & A. Sauvage. Éditions Sociales, 1963.

5. ——— — ed. G. Sablayrolles. Classiques Larousse, 1965.

Background Studies

6. Adam, Antoine — *Histoire de la littérature française au 17e siècle*. Domat, 1962, 5 vols (vol. 3).

7. Bergson, Henri — *Le Rire. Essai sur la signification du comique*. P.U.F., 1940 [1900].

8. La Grange — *Le Registre de La Grange, 1659-1685*, eds. B. E. & G. P. Young. Geneva: Slatkine, 1977.

9. Lancaster, H. C. — *A History of French Dramatic Literature in the Seventeenth Century*. Baltimore/London: Johns Hopkins U.P., 1929-42, 10 vols (Part III: 'The Period of Molière').

10. Mongrédien,G. (ed.) — *Recueil des textes et documents du XVIIe siècle relatifs à Molière*. CNRS, 1966.

11. Rousseau, J.-J. — *Lettre à D'Alembert sur les spectacles* (1758), ed. M. Fuchs. Geneva: Droz, 'Textes Littéraires Français', 1948.

Studies on *Le Misanthrope*

12. Arnavon, Jacques — *'Le Misanthrope' de Molière*. Plon, 1930.

13. Comédie-Française — nos.131-2, Sept-Oct. 1984.

14. Coquelin, Constant — *Molière et 'Le Misanthrope'*. Ollendorff, 1881.

15. Doumic, René — *'Le Misanthrope' de Molière*. Éditions Mellottée, 1930.

16. Horville, Robert — *Le Misanthrope*. Hatier, 'Profil d'une Œuvre', 1981.

17. Jasinski, René — *Molière et 'Le Misanthrope'*. Armand Colin, 1951.

18. Vincent, Jean-Pierre — *Alceste et l'absolutisme*. Galilée, 1977.

Studies on Molière

19. Arnavon, Jacques — *Notes sur l'interprétation de Molière*. Plon, 1923.

20. Bray, René — *Molière, homme de théâtre*. Mercure de France, 1954.

21. Collinet, Jean-Pierre — *Lectures de Molière*. Armand Colin, 1974.

22. Defaux, Gérard — *Molière ou les métamorphoses du comique*. Lexington, Kentucky: French Forum, 1980.

23. Descotes, Maurice — *Les Grands Rôles du théâtre de Molière*. P.U.F., 1960.

24. Fernandez, Ramon — *La Vie de Molière*. Gallimard, 1929.

25. Grimarest — *La Vie de Monsieur de Molière (1705)*. Renaissance du Livre, 1930.

26. Guicharnaud, J. — *Molière, une aventure théâtrale*. Gallimard, 1963.

27. Herzel, Roger W. — *Molière's Actors: a Reconstruction of the Original Casting of the Plays of Molière*. Cornell Univ., Ph.D., 1974.

28. Howarth,W. D. — *Molière. A Playwright and his Audience*. Cambridge: University Press, 1982.

29. Hubert, J. D. — *Molière and the comedy of intellect*. Berkeley: Univ. of California Press, 1962.

30. Michaut, Gustave — *Les Luttes de Molière*. Hachette, 1925.

31. Moore, W. G. *Molière. A new criticism.* Oxford: Clarendon Press, 1949.

Articles

32. Brody, Jacques '*Dom Juan* and *Le Misanthrope:* the aesthetics of individualism in Molière', *PMLA,* 84 (1969), 559-76.

33. Cismaru, Alfred '*Les Sincères* and *Le Misanthrope:* an attempt to settle the relationship', *French Review,* 42 (1969), 865-70.

34. Defaux, Gérard 'Alceste et les rieurs', *Revue d'Histoire Littéraire de la France,* 74, no. 4 (1974), 579-99.

35. Delon, Michel 'Lectures de Molière au 18e siècle', *Europe,* 523-4 (1972), 92-101.

36. Descotes, Maurice 'Nouvelles interprétations moliéresques', *Œuvres et Critiques,* VI, 1 (1981), pp.33-55.

37. Gossip, C.J. 'The Initial Success of *Le Misanthrope*', *French Studies,* 39, 2 (1985), 143-51.

38. Gossman, Lionel 'Molière's *Misanthrope:* melancholy & society in the age of the counterreformation', *Theatre Journal,* 34, no. 3 (1982), 323-43.

39. Gutwirth, M. 'Visages d'Alceste', *Œuvres et Critiques,* VI, 1 (1981), 77-89.

40. Hall, Gaston 'The literary context of Molière's *Le Misanthrope*', *Studi francesi,* 14 (1970), 20-38.

41. Herzel, Roger W. 'Much depends on the Acting: The Original Cast of *Le Misanthrope*', *PMLA,* 95 (1980), 348-66.

42. Hope, Quentin M. 'Society in *Le Misanthrope*', *French Review,* 32 (1959), 329-36.

43. Horville, Robert 'La Cohérence des dénouements de *Tartuffe,* de *Dom Juan* et du *Misanthrope*', *Revue d'Histoire du Théâtre,* 26 (1974), 240-5.

44. Howarth, W. D. 'Alceste ou l'honnête homme imaginaire', *Revue d'Histoire du Théâtre,* 26 (1974), 93-102.

45. Lawrence, F. L. 'Our Alceste or Molière's?', *Revue des Langues Vivantes,* 38 (1972), 477-91.

46. Lawrenson, T. E. 'The wearing o' the green: yet another look at "l'homme aux rubans verts"', in Howarth & Thomas (eds.), *Molière Stage and Study: Essays in*

Honour of W. G. Moore, Oxford: Clarendon, 1973, pp. 163-9.

47. Lindsay, F. W. 'Alceste and the sonnet', *French Review,* 28 (1954-55), 395-402.

48. McBride, Robert 'From Inflation to Deflation: Molière's Changing Vision of Court Life', *Seventeenth-Century French Studies,* 10 (1988), 53-71.

49. Mesnard, Jean '*Le Misanthrope:* mise en question de l'art de plaire', *Revue d'Histoire Littéraire de la France,* 72 (1972), 863-89.

50. Peacock, Noël 'Verbal Costume in *Le Misanthrope*', *Seventeenth-Century French Studies,* 9 (1987), 74-93.

51. ———— 'Lessons unheeded: The Dénouement of *Le Misanthrope*', *Nottingham French Studies,* 29, 2 (1990), 10-20.

52. Picard, Michel 'Le Personnage d'Alceste dans *Le Misanthrope* de Molière', *L'Information Littéraire,* 9 (1957), 134-7.

53. Robert, R. 'Des commentaires de première main sur les chefs-d'œuvre les plus discutés de Molière', *Revue des Sciences Humaines,* 81 (1956), 19-53.

54. Rojtman, Betty 'Alceste dans le théâtre de Molière', *Revue d'Histoire Littéraire de la France,* 73 (1973), 963-81.

55. Shepherd, James 'Arsinoé as Puppeteer', *French Review,* 42 (1968), 262-71.

56. Thomas, Merlin 'Philinte and Éliante', in Howarth & Thomas (eds.), *Molière Stage and Study,* pp. 73-92.

57. Yarrow, P.J. 'A Reconsideration of Alceste', *French Studies,* 13 (1959), 314-29.